HOW TO GET TO
THE TOP

D0170562

ALSO BY JEFFREY J. FOX

HOW TO GET TO

THE TOP

Business Lessons

Learned

at the

Dinner Table

JEFFREY J. FOX

New York

Copyright © 2007 Jeffrey J. Fox

Library of Congress Cataloging-in-Publication Data

Fox, Jeffrey J.
   How to get to the top : business lessons learned at the dinner table / Jeffrey J. Fox.
       p.   cm.
ISBN-10: 1-4013-0330-7
ISBN-13: 978-1-4013-0330-3
1. Success in business.   2. Business etiquette.   3. Customer relations.
4. Career development.   I. Title.   II. Title: Business lessons learned at the dinner table.

HF5386.F527   2007
658.4'09—dc22

                                                              2006053155

FIRST EDITION

10 9 8 7 6 5 4 3 2 1

This book is dedicated to the
Fabulous, Fantastic Fox Family:
Marlene, Erin, Damian, Brenna Rose,
Luca Modesto, Ella, Heather, Chris,
and more on the way.
All the other Foxes and Flahertys
can also consider themselves dedicatees.
Given!

CONTENTS

Contents

Contents

Contents

{ **xi** }

Contents

ACKNOWLEDGMENTS

Thanks to—

Each of the superstar contributors (see pages 173–204) and, with reverence, to the contributors' parents, grandparents, teachers, and mentors. The readers and students of management and entrepreneurship owe you.

Brenda Copeland, executive editor at Hyperion, who made some big-league improvements to this book. And thanks to the classy Hyperion team who makes these books possible.

Doris Michaels of the DSM Literary Agency in New York City, who is literally a world-class literary agent. And to DSM agent Delia Berrigan Fakis, who will make this book available around the world.

Those friends who get an early look and better the book.

HOW TO GET TO
THE TOP

FOREWORD

*T*he kitchen table is the iconic American center of the family household. It is where boys and girls learn, get ambition, get confidence, get ready, get the spunk to make it to the top. The kitchen table, or its equivalent, has been the center of families of all cultures in all places since the cavemen discovered fire.

Dinner at home is spring training for dinners of importance conducted elsewhere. It is at dinner where blessings are offered, toasts made, manners learned, issues discussed. It is at the dinner table where business and life lessons are learned by millions of boys and girls that will get them to the top in all possible careers. It is at the dinner table where business is learned, conducted, completed. It is during dinner that wisdom, experience, and the history of elders is passed.

This book is based on the life-forming remembrances of people who made it to the top.

Now raise a glass to parents, grandparents, dinner partners everywhere: "To your health and happiness . . . and thank you."

When Thomas Jefferson
Dined Alone

*T*here are two times when you must have perfect table manners: when you dine with others and when you dine alone. Be it a family meal,
a business meeting, a campfire roast, dining with
others is a linchpin of civilization. The table is
where partnerships begin, plans are laid, decisions
made, information exchanged, deals struck. A person's natural conduct at the table is often a window
into the persona. Is he or she well-taught, polite,
attentive, funny, observant, disciplined? Or indul-
gent, sloppy, avaricious, uncouth, rude, inappro-
priate?

Poor table manners are a sign of self-absorption
and an insensitivity to others. There is nothing

gained by poor table manners. Thus, it is always a social sin to eat like a hog. The same is true when dining alone. Show yourself the same respect and dignity you show others. During World War II, while in prisoner-of-war camps, British army officers insisted that soldiers of all rank, despite deplorable conditions, maintain acceptable table manners. Such rigor reminded the men of their humanity and superiority of spirit.

Dining alone reminds everyone of President John F. Kennedy's 1962 speech honoring America's Nobel Prize winners. Kennedy welcomed the Nobel winners, members of Congress, and esteemed guests noting, "This is the most extraordinary collection of talent, of human knowledge, that has ever been gathered together at the White House, with the possible exception of when Thomas Jefferson dined alone."

Be assured that when the great Thomas Jefferson dined alone, civility was not in peril.

Hire a Helicopter

*I*t was Saturday. The offices were closed for the weekend. The only person in the building was Guiseppe Italo, whose job was sorting and delivering the company mail. Guiseppe did not have to be in the building that Saturday afternoon and he had little in his life but the mailroom job. But he loved his company and just liked being in the offices. He had worked for his company for over thirty years in such jobs as driver, gofer, landscaping, office cleaning, maintenance. The only employee who wore a company work shirt, which he proudly wore with his name stenciled on a pocket, Joe was full of company lore and stories. He had heard a lot, seen a lot, and he never spoke a disloyal word. Joe had seen people come and go, and he'd seen young, eager, hardworking people progress from trainee to president. In fact, he now worked a few layers of management below one of those eager hotshots. Joe liked this hotshot, who always addressed him by name, always sincerely asked how he was doing, and had arranged a surprise $500 bonus with a note that read, "Joe: You don't have to, but thanks for always putting your company's interests before yours. *Signature.*" That framed note hung in the mailroom.

It was late that Saturday afternoon when Joe heard a phone ringing somewhere in the building. At first, Joe ignored the ringing. Then he realized the call had somehow bypassed the switchboard and was ringing on someone's direct line. Joe went to find the ringing phone. The phone kept ringing. Joe later said, "That ringing phone sounded real desperate." Joe found the phone after twenty-five or thirty rings.

"How may I help you?" asked Joe.

"I'm so glad you're there. I was just about to hang up. We need some help," said the caller.

"Okay, what's up?" asked Joe.

"We will run out of your product in about three hours. If we run out, our production line will shut down. If the line shuts down, it will cost us hundreds of thousands of dollars an hour, and my boss and I will be in big trouble. The product we need is your BRF1984. Can we get some?" asked the caller.

"I think we might have some trade show samples, stuff used for training, that kind of thing. I can't promise, but maybe we can find something."

Joe got the caller's name, number, address, approximate amount of product needed. Joe told the caller he would see what he could do and get back to him.

"We will be grateful," said the caller. "By the way, what's your name?"

Joe called the hotshot at home. He explained the problem. He told the exec that he had prowled the building and had scavenged product from the product manager's office, from the lab, from the packaging department.

"Joe, I've never heard of Factory Town, New York. Where is it?"

"It is about a hundred seventy miles as the crow flies from the office," answered Joe. "Real far by car."

"We'll never get the stuff there in time," said the hotshot.

"I have a suggestion," said Joe.

"Hit me!"

"We could hire a private plane or a helicopter," said Joe.

Two hours later a helicopter landed in front of a factory in Factory Town, New York.

Joe was a talker. By nine o'clock Monday morning the helicopter story had made its way to the company's CEO and chairman. The chairman was a decent guy, but a notorious tightfisted skinflint. He hated to spend money, let alone spend money profligately. At 9:10 a.m. the hotshot was on his way to the chairman's office.

"Is it true you told Joe it was okay to order a helicopter to fly from here to someplace in upstate New York?" asked the chairman.

"Yes," answered the hotshot.

"How much did it cost?" asked the chairman.

"I don't know."

"You don't know? What do you mean you don't know?"

"I told Joe to have them bill us," said the hotshot.

"Bill us?" blurted the chairman.

At that moment, the chairman's longtime assistant walked in and told him there was an important caller on the line and he should take it. The chairman picked up the phone and listened in astonishment as the caller said: "Mr. Chairman. My name is [withheld]. I am president of [a U.S. automobile manufacturer]. I was told that you have a guy working there who saved my company maybe millions of dollars. I think his name is Joe Italo, or something like that. Please bill us for the helicopter, and be assured we will never forget what you did for us."

"Thank you very much," said the chairman.

"No, we thank you," said the customer.

The chairman looked at the ceiling, asking no

one, "Guiseppe, why on earth were you here on Saturday afternoon?" He turned to his assistant. "Ask Joe if he would please come up here." He looked at the hotshot. "Knowing Joe, he'll be here in a heartbeat. Any suggestions?"

"Ask him about the helicopter. He flew back and forth in it," said the hotshot.

The chairman stared in dismay.

Hiring a helicopter to save a customer can make a career. (Hiring a helicopter to visit the casinos can sink a career.) Hire a helicopter if you want to fly high.

· III ·

Juggle Like
Mom

*M*oms who work have a tough job—actually two tough jobs. Single moms have two super-tough jobs. Just like the Richter scale of escalating earthquake magnitudes, the more kids in the family, the tougher the job. Whatever their title or responsibilities at work, single moms are always the CEO, at the top of their families. (Actually in 98 percent plus of all families, single or not, moms are the CEO.) As CEO of their families, moms do more tasks, make more decisions, solve more problems, deal with more crises in one week than even the hardest-working, most hands-on corporate CEO will handle in a Galapagos tortoise's lifetime. (And every single CEO or CMO or president or C of anything who was raised by a single mom will so attest.)

Growing up with a single mom, observing a single mom, remembering with hindsight a single mom is worth 100 credits at every one of the best graduate business schools on terra firma. A single mom's typical weekly "to do" list (each "to do" multiplied by the number of kids) would minimally include: money earning, bill paying, meal planning, grocery shopping, meal making, lunch packing, clothes selection, clothes cleaning, homework checking, bath taking, teeth brushing, schedule meshing, bed making, chore assigning, teacher meetings, after-school pickups, latchkey hiding, babysitter interviewing and reference checking and hiring and training and paying and monitoring and firing, story reading, house cleaning, juggling, juggling, and too much more.

Single moms are more than the CEO of their families. They are saleswomen, selling their kids on washing the dishes, taking out the trash, doing their homework. On kids cleaning their rooms, smart moms backpedal. Bad ROT (see Chapter XVII).

Like sales managers holding up Kevlar umbrellas shielding the salespeople from the nonsense thrown from above, moms struggling financially protect their kids from the scary reality of their plight. They are chief financial officers, balancing the checkbook, juggling which bill to pay when. They are the human resources directors, helping their kids cope with middle school, with taunters and teasers, with braces, with college applications. They are operations managers, getting each kid to soccer, or piano, or gymnastics on time every time.

Moms have every job at home that exists in every good organization. Single moms are an ever-onstage, no-day-off, all-star ensemble cast of provider, ringmaster, nurturer, doctor, nurse, example setter, bar raiser, coach, mentor, teacher, shielder, protector, corrector, applauder, chef, chauffer, pain duller, smile maker, hugger.

Moms are always valuable employees. They work extra hard because they know that sometimes they have to put a sick child first, and they don't want such occasions to threaten their job. Single moms are valuable employees because they are experts at getting things done, moving things along, making compromises, making decisions.

To get to the top, juggle like Mom. Meticulously manage your time. Keep a list. Stay organized. Be relentless. Get a lot done every day. Plan. Be on time. Stay healthy. Don't complain.

Be like Mom: No matter the pain, don't complain. As one at the top puts it: "In all the years, over forty, that my mother was a single mom, despite poverty, crippling ailments, heartbreaking setbacks, the one thing my mother never once did was to complain. Not once."

IV

Be Both Mr. Inside and Mr. Outside

*1*944, 1945, and 1946 were glory years for Army, the U.S. Military Academy's football team. Army was undefeated: twenty-seven wins and one tie. Army was a powerhouse. Providing the power were Felix "Doc" Blanchard and Glenn Davis, both great running backs. Both players won the Heisman Trophy given to college football's best player. The media nicknamed Blanchard and Davis Mr. Inside and Mr. Outside. Doc Blanchard, Mr. Inside, was a fullback. He was a bruising, powerful fellow who ran inside, up the middle, through the line. Glenn Davis, Mr. Outside, was a lightning-fast halfback who broke long touchdowns by getting to the outside, outside the line, and outrunning the defense. These two men were leaders: They led their teams to victory, and later had leadership careers in the military and in business.

Leaders of companies, of organizations, must be both Mr. (or Ms.) Inside and Mr. (or Ms.) Outside. You are Mr. Inside when you are inside the company working with colleagues. You are Mr. Outside when you are outside the company meeting with customers, with distributors, with retailers, with shareholders, suppliers, and the media.

As Mr. Inside, you are modest, humble, collegial, courteous, calm, controlled (not controlling), questioning, inspecting, helpful. You help others solve problems. You remove barriers and frustrations that hinder people in doing their jobs. You give credit and recognition and thank-yous.

When you are Mr. Outside, you are a flag-waving company patriot. You promote your company, your products, services, and values. You do not promote yourself (unless you are the product or a spokesperson for the product). You do not get your picture on the cover of a magazine; you get your product's picture on the cover. You are a tireless, fearless, enthusiastic, positive seller of your company. You sell, ask for the business, attract investors, get and keep customers, influence influencers.

Inside, you lead from the middle. You are the hub of the wheel. You sell inside, persuading employees to change, to innovate, to improve, to learn, to serve customers better.

Outside, you lead in front. You are in touch with customers. You set the example for other employees. You are the way. You show the way . . . for customers and employees.

When you are both Mr. Inside and Mr. Outside, you are leading and motivating.

You can start running hard and fast the day you join a company. Be Mr. Inside/Mr. Outside now. You can run inside and outside in your organization no matter your job or rank or seniority. Don't wait until you get the big job, the big promotion. If you wait to run, you may be waiting for your entire career.

V

"What I Would Do in
the First 100 Days"

Someday you want to be CEO, or president, or global director of this or that, or vice president of sales, or head of manufacturing. For whatever legitimate reasons, you are not a realistic candidate for that job. That's okay. You are ambitious, but you are a realist. In addition to doing your job as well as it can be done, you are always thinking about how your company can be better. You don't publicly criticize management. You don't participate in bitch sessions. You stay out of office politics. You are a worker. You are a thinker. You keep a file or a notebook or an "Alive Sea Scroll" of your ideas. You are always thinking: "If I were CEO, what would I do to increase revenues, increase profits, cut costs, slaughter competition?" You have ideas on what you would do, why you would do it, a thoughtful consideration of all possible consequences, facts, numbers, data.

A new CEO is installed. The CEO may know you, of you, or not. After the new CEO catches his or her breath, which may take a day or a month, you send the CEO a memo titled, "What I Would Do in the First 100 Days If I Were CEO." In this memo you list your ideas, from one to whatever. List only your ideas. Don't include your rationale or analysis. Save your arguments and homework for a possible meeting with the new CEO. Be sure your memo is polite, nonjudgmental, noncritical. Knock no one. You have nothing to lose, and a lot to gain. (In good companies information flows in any direction regardless of the chain of command. Decisions, of course, go through the chain of command.) You will gain the attention of the CEO. You will be seen as creative, thoughtful, a company loyalist. You might be consulted. You will go on the CEO's list of possible impact players. You will be evaluated.

Your list might include ideas for new products, new brand names, strategy changes or additions, acquisitions or divestitures, new sales force compensation schemes, new processes to reduce waste or increase yield, consolidation of redundant functions or facilities, strategic partners to cultivate, strategic customers to get and keep, solutions for big problems, ways to ignite sales.

Good companies love good ideas. But what they love more are profitable, affordable, doable ways to implement those good ideas. Good companies are always looking to identify impact people who can turn ideas into money. The "100 Days" memo puts you into that rare census of employees who are both innovative and thinking about how to implement the innovations.

To get to the top you have to think as if you were on top. Your first priority is to do your job superbly, keep the cash register ringing, the innovations flowing, and unnecessary costs a go-going.

You will be the only person in your company to send a "100 Days" memo.

"See That Shack
Over There . . ."

After the tenth and twentieth and hundredth time, his kids would respond with a roll of the eyes, perhaps a sarcastic, non-heartfelt "ha ha," or with a "Dad, that is so old, and so not funny, and so insensitive to the misfortunes of others. Get over it." Mom would smile and shake her head.

Undaunted, unswayed by the family, whatever the trip, wherever the drive, whenever Dad spotted an unkempt house, with unnecessary junk decorating the yard, he would always, unalterably, undifferentingly warn his children: "See that shack over there? That's where you'll be living if you don't study, if you don't work hard, and if you don't save some money." Then Dad would launch into his sermon. "Not having money does not mean you are poor. Not having money means you're broke. Many people who have no money are rich of mind, rich in spirit. Having no money does not mean you should have no pride. A homeless person can be neat and dignified. Relisten to Dolly Parton's classic 'A Coat of Many Colors' to understand how the poor can be rich. But whoever is living in that place doesn't care, doesn't work hard. That house is a portrait of laziness. That house, with its washable windows, pullable weeds, cuttable grass, removable trash is a disgrace. The owners or renters or squatters there are shameful."

Mom sighed. The kids sighed.

But books were studied. Classes attended. Jobs gotten. Bank accounts opened. Weeds pulled.

"See that prison chain gang over there picking up stuff on the highway . . . ?"

Dad never stopped pointing out the consequences of sloth and quitting.

Don't Put General Patton in Charge of the Mess Hall

Would any good commander put his best battle-wise infantry general in charge of the mess hall, or in charge of supplies, instead of fighting the enemy? The answer is no. General Patton will fight the war because he is the best general to fight the war. Other guys are best at logistics or recruiting or espionage or running the military hospitals. These jobs are critical to the success of the army, to the defense of the country, and the guys best at those jobs must do those jobs.

You must do the same in your organization. Put those people who are best at scoring goals up front, and those best at stopping goals on defense, or in the goal. Put people who are best at selling into sales, and people who can keep books into accounting.

In all organizations there is an ever-present temptation, and often inarguable need, to go to the go-to guy or gal who can solve the problem, make something happen, get it done. A super customer service person is asked to manage a crucial voice-of-the-customer market research study, stealing him from making customers' problems go away. A super seller is asked to help collect big unpaid bills, stealing her from signing up new customers, making new deals, ringing the cash register. Don't dilute your army. Don't divert your soldiers.

Don't put your General Patton in charge of the cafeteria. Put your generals in charge of getting and keeping profitable customers.

Ah-ten-hut!

• VIII •

Pick Up the Check for Clergy,
Teachers, and Soldiers

*I*f you can afford it, and you see some of your old schoolteachers having dinner in the local trattoria, pick up their check as a partial thank-you for having helped you learn to read and write. If you see two clergymen having dinner, pick up their check. It's a pittance of thanks to men and women who have devoted their lives to God and to others. If you see five soldiers having a beer, get their check. You owe them.

It's best to pay their checks anonymously. Giving back is good for business. Try it. You will see an immediate improvement in your personal and business life.

IX

Unlearn the
Bad ABC's

*D*on't be angry, or quick to anger. Don't ac-cuse. Don't blame. Don't criticize. Don't complain.

Anger impairs judgment. Acting on anger is of-ten regretted. Stay calm. Look confident. Friends, fellow workers, investors, partners want to do busi-ness with the continuously cool, not with seethers, not with screamers.

A person is either guilty or not. Based on facts, you know if the person is guilty, or you don't. If the person is guilty, present the facts and execute your remedy. If you suspect the person is guilty, don't accuse; gather more facts. If you accuse a guilty person without proof, you alert without gain. Accusing gets you nothing.

Blaming is a worthless activity. If someone made a mistake, they didn't do so on purpose. Clean up the mess; then do whatever is needed to prevent its reoccurrence.

There is no such thing as "constructive criticism." Criticism is always a negative, and is always taken as negative by the criticized. When someone says, "Would you like some constructive criticism?" the other person immediately thinks, "No. I would rather eat raw chicken." Don't criticize. Make suggestions, coach, give tips, demonstrate, show techniques, provide examples, set examples. Leave the joy of criticism to those lovable pundits and columnists who themselves can't cook a soufflé, or create a Hemingway-like Santiago, compose a *Cats,* hit a major league fastball, or run a business.

No one likes complainers, whiners, excuse makers. No one wants to work or do business with a complainer. Complainers are drainers.

Complainers drain energy, time, fun. (An honest complaint, as in customer complaint, is okay, sought, welcomed, vanquished.) Don't complain about a problem: Do something to make the problem go bye-bye.

"Now you know my ABC's, won't you come and work with me?"

X

Always Compliment the Chef . . .
Especially at Home

People who complain about how tough their jobs are, are sometimes admonished: "If you can't stand the heat, get out of the kitchen." That suggestion rings true because it is hot in the kitchen. In most busy kitchens, with stoves and ovens going full blast, it is so sweltering that the frantically working cooks guzzle ice water all day and night. A chef's work environment is a minefield of boiling water, hissing steam, sharp knives, red-hot burners, slippery floors, scalding pans. A chef who prepares 100 dishes meets 100 deadlines. A chef who prepares 100 dishes gets graded, rated, praised, panned 100 times. Some chefs are celebrities, but in 99 percent of all restaurants on 99 percent of all nights, a chef labors invisibly, incognito, unacknowledged. The only time chefs are recognized is the rare time they turn risotto into rocks, or soufflés into cement. These hard-working men and women spend hours chopping, peeling, mincing, slicing, dicing, sautéing, baking, roasting, freezing. And at midnight these unknown toilers toss their aprons, wash their hands, head for home. Generally, a thankless job unless you send a compliment. The good chef is anonymous.

But not anonymous at home!

At home the chef is well-known. The chef is Mom or Dad, wife or husband. The at-home chef goes to the grocery store, lugs the bags, puts stuff away, prepares the food, cooks the dishes, serves the meal, clears the table, does the dishes. Okay, Mom or Dad doesn't do all these activities all the time, but they do all of them lots of times! And these chefs rarely get a standing ovation, a curtain call.

Although a botched dish can darken the dining, a wonderful meal can make good things happen. A chef may be your silent partner in doing business, calming a customer, recruiting a super-star. Your home chef will participate in discussing business, making decisions, giving advice, listening to problems, softening the blows of daily life. A wonderful dinner, out or at home, facilitates conversation, facilitates deal making. A wonderful meal can make the memory that cements the deal, makes the occasion unforgettable. If you have an unforgettable meal, don't forget to compliment the chef.

Always compliment the chef. He or she earned the compliment. It's a classy sign of respect, rarely done, a point of difference, and never forgotten. If you have an unforgettable meal, like last night or tonight, don't forget to compliment the chef, especially the chef at home. Lord knows, he or she has earned it.

Standing, clapping, stamping, whistling, raising a glass in modest appreciation for a modest meal is never over the top for even the most modest of at-home chefs.

Sometimes over the top is the way to the top.

Speak Sweetly: You May Have to Eat Your Words

*T*he old English proverb "Sticks and stones will break my bones, but names will never hurt me" is only half-right. Being called a "name," such as "tub of lard," is hurtful, and every kid and every adult knows it. So be nice. It costs nothing. Don't use bad words on others, especially people you don't know, that you wouldn't want used on you, or against you. Don't get caught in the "I'm the perfect preacher, politician" trap. It is common for the self-righteous to rail against sin and sinners and enemies, promising all types of gruesome punishment. And it is also common for a righteous soul to find himself in a compromised position . . . staring straight at the same forty lashes he prescribed for others.

Don't yell at a colleague. Tomorrow she could be your boss. Don't brag and boast. Today's loser might be tomorrow's big winner . . . over you. Don't talk down to people. You may be looking up someday.

History is replete with market share leaders dismissive of the upstart, only to get pounded by the upstart (read Toyota and GM; read Apple and IBM PC). The advent of the FOX News Channel was disdainfully dissed by a competitor's COΛ (chief of arrogance): "We'll squash them [FOX] like a bug." Well, that bug could bite, and a decade later the COA's network is the squashee.

Movie aficionados believe that some of the best dialogue to ever make it to the big screen is what the unmatchable Elmore Leonard wrote for *Hombre*. Barbara Rush plays the imperial Audra Favor. Paul Newman is John Russell, the hombre. When they first meet, Audra Favor oozes with disdain for the hombre and his people, Apache

Indians. Especially repugnant to her is the practice of eating dogs, and she says so.

AUDRA FAVOR: I wouldn't care how hungry I got. I know I wouldn't eat one of those camp dogs.

JOHN RUSSELL: You'd eat it. You'd fight for the bones, too.

AUDRA FAVOR: Have you ever eaten a dog, Mr. Russell?

JOHN RUSSELL: Eaten one and lived like one.

Later, Audra is kidnapped by the bad guys, tied to a post, starved for days. As Audra pleads for help, the hombre tells one of the good guys, "Ask her if she'll eat dog now."

Speak sweetly, not harshly. Speak sweetly, no matter your ire, no matter your cause, no matter your exalted or leadership position. Speak sweetly, you may have to eat your words. You may not like the taste of nasty words, unless, of course, you prefer dog.

· XII ·

Don't Mope

*T*o mope is to be gloomy, dejected; to brood, to sulk. To "mope around" is to amble listlessly and aimlessly. A moper, or mope, is a drag. Everybody hates to be around a mope. It is depressing. Mopes are wet blankets, dark clouds. Friends, family, customers, colleagues, partners want to be with people who have zest, energy, "joie de vivre."

Moping is a waste of time and a waste of life. Moping steals from action. It steals from accomplishing. You can't get things done in a state of mopitry.

Moping is not the blues. Moping is not clinical depression. To mope is a deliberate decision.

(Moping is a selfish decision. Clinical depression is not. Depression must be treated by doctors.) Because a person is bored or upset or spoiled or has a run of bad luck, he decides to mope. Teenagers are excellent mopers, but they are not alone. Sulking after rejection, or after a thoughtless act, or after a thoughtless "gift," is not an uncommon phenomenon. It is normal to be down after a loss or disappointment, but the loss was yesterday.

Don't mope. Don't mope around. Skip around. Jog around the block. Action trumps moping every time.

· XIII ·

No One Cares About Technology

*H*igh tech! Early adopters brag about it. Engineers spout it. Venture capitalists invest in it. Insecure salespeople hide behind its jargon. Weak advertising agencies describe it with acronyms and goofy vocab. Silly brand names denote it. High technology. It's one of the holy grails of business. It's today's talkies.

High tech is great . . . except for one small caveat: Customers don't care about technology. Customers don't care one megabit about technology. Customers don't buy technology; they buy what they get from technology. Banks don't buy automatic teller machines; they buy reduced labor costs. End-user consumers don't care how an

ATM works. They just want to put in an encoded piece of plastic (high tech?) and receive error-free, accurately counted pieces of non-duplicable paper (high tech?) to use to purchase a magnetic ink cartridge for their printer. People don't care how a fax machine works. They don't care how e-mail works. They don't care how a CAT scanner scans, or what MRI means, or how a cell phone calls and receives. No one on the planet cares! Customers just want to push the little green icon and call Mom in Istanbul.

That customers don't care about technology is hard for lots of companies and marketers to bite, chew, swallow, digest. These product makers use technical language and novel product features to shield themselves from customer query and customer appraisal. For some sellers it is safer to be smarter than the customer than it is to deal with customer objections and price concerns.

Take the case of two fellows competing to sell an MRI machine to a large private hospital. Each works for a world-class company. After a number of successful meetings with the hospital's doctors and technical people, each salesperson was scheduled to meet with the hospital's CEO, chief of the medical staff, CFO, and chief technology officer. The price of the MRI machines ranged from three to four million dollars. The top executives who managed the hospital had somewhat unusual backgrounds for people in the health care industry. Except for the chief of staff, none were doctors, nor did they have deep experience running other hospitals or medical-related companies. The CEO was from the hotel and entertainment industry.

The first salesperson presented what he called the "total deck" on his company, his machine, his technology. The "total deck" was over 100 PowerPoint slides detailing the number of manufacturing plants around the world, the number of employees, the numbers of PhD researchers, the magnets, the pixels, the imaging science. "I'd rather be squeezed by a thirty-foot-long Indian python than go through this again," the CEO thought to himself.

The second salesperson showed up with a slim

notebook. He started the meeting by saying, "This should only take about thirty minutes. The primary purpose is to show you how much money you will generate from your investment in our MRI machine, okay?" The CEO nodded.

The salesman continued, "Your technical experts have been to other customer sites and have seen the machine in action. Your staff is completely comfortable with the quality of the images, the service package, and the training. Is that correct, Doctor?" The chief of staff nodded.

The salesman continued, "The average net revenue to the hospital for this type of MRI procedure is eighteen hundred dollars. Would you be interested in what other good hospitals are doing to maximize patient usage of their machines, and how much total revenue you can expect per year?" The CEO nodded.

The salesman handed everyone a folder. "These are a conservative and an aggressive pro forma estimate of how many procedures you can expect, and how insurance and Medicare reimbursements will impact your revenues. The bottom line is that your hospital should do at least thirty MRIs a week, or fifteen hundred the first year. This represents a revenue stream of $2,700,000. The operating costs are detailed in the pro formas. You will recoup your investment around month seventeen. How does this sound?"

The CEO thought to himself, "We can jam a lot more patients through this beast than those puny numbers."

The CFO said, "Four million dollars is a big number. We don't have that amount of cash available to make an outright purchase."

The salesperson responded, "If my company were able to finance the purchase, using our credit and leasing division, would that be a way to go?" The CFO nodded.

The salesman then said, "It is costing you fifty-four thousand dollars a week to go without this MRI machine. If you agree, you will get a financing proposal tomorrow, and an operating machine in four weeks. Can you give me the go-ahead?" And the salesperson kept quiet until the CEO nodded one more time.

After the salesperson left, the CEO turned to his associates and asked, "Can these machines really see inside people using magnets?"

Don't depend on the technology, no matter how novel, how marvelous, to sell itself. Nothing sells itself. The formula for new product success is 2 percent technology and 98 percent marketing. Even the most sophisticated customers don't care about technology. The product delivers or it doesn't. The customer gets the performance and quality he expects or he doesn't purchase.

• XIV •

Quality Is Not
Job 1

Despite the proclamations of the venerable Ford Motor Company, quality is not Job 1. Marketing is Job 1. Marketing: The identification, attraction, getting, and keeping of profitable customers is Job 1. Selling is part of marketing and is part of Job 1. Explaining and demonstrating quality is part of Job 1. So, too, are innovations, pre-deadline delivery, friendly customer service, and products priced to value. These requirements are part of Job 1.

Quality is part of Job 1, but not the way Ford sees it. *Quality* is a meaningless word. Quality is defined by the customer, not by the manufacturer or seller. Regardless of the requisite engineering ingenuity or milestone research, a million-mile bearing is not "better quality" than a hundred-mile bearing if the customer wants a hundred-mile bearing. "Better quality" is not a ten-second curing glue if the customer wants a thirty-second curing glue. An international phone that has twenty features no one uses is not superior to a phone that has three oft-used features.

There is no point in advertising your view of your product's quality. Quality is expected by the customer. Acceptable quality is necessary to just get in the game. Acceptable quality is a basic rudimentary business criteria. The customer's definition of quality is relative. A five-dollar cheeseburger may be of outstanding quality, and a fifty-dollar steak may not.

Quality is not Job 1. A keen and clear understanding of what quality the customer expects, and delivering that quality at a price-to-value the customer will pay, and doing so every time is part of Job 1. Selling a bait pail of one hundred worms, of which only one catches a fish, is wicked good quality to a five-year-old. Selling one million vehicle brake systems, of which one fails, probably won't get a check in the "good quality" box by the dear and departed.

Good customers will pay for good quality. And good customers will roll with you. If your quality falters or falls below acceptable, good customers will not immediately stampede for the egress. Good customers are forgiving, flexible, forward thinking. If you are fair, customers will be fair.

Calling or branding your business or product as "quality this" or "quality that" (as in Quality Motel) is mumbling underwater. Having the "best quality" is worthless if no one buys. If you want an opinion on your quality, your customer will let you know.

Getting the customer to purchase your product, and to repeat that purchase is Job 1.

XV

Tip As If You
Were the Tippee

People who earn their living by earning tips or gratuities need those tips to live. There are countless jobs where tips are an important component of total compensation. Taxi drivers, valets, baggage handlers, bellmen, waiters, waitresses, paperboys, caddies, shoe shiners, shuttle drivers, concierges, delivery people, hairdressers, doormen, bartenders, barbers, babysitters are compensated in part, or in total, with tips.

It is rare when a tippee does not earn the tip. Never does a hardworking, honest tippee not earn his or her tip. Depending on the country, the culture, depending on the job or task, everybody knows that some part of the final bill includes a tip. To not tip is to not really pay the person for the job.

Imagine you were the tippee stiffed by a cheap tipper. Imagine you sorted, tagged, and loaded ten pieces of luggage for a "We're late. We're in a hurry" couple on their way to Bermuda only to get an over-the-shoulder wave as they pranced into the airport. Imagine you were the babysitter who changed two diapers, cleaned up the dog's mess, put away a million toys, and, while being short-tipped by the mother, you were told, "You only worked two hours and fifty minutes."

There is another universe of tippees. This universe includes business owners, corporate executives, Wall Street operators, factory workers, customer service representatives, office workers, nurses, athletes, entrepreneurs. The "tips" these folks get are delicately called bonuses, signing bonuses, completion bonuses, finder's fees, profit sharing, referral fees, stock options, stock grants, incentive compensation, commissions, perquisites. These tippees earn their tips for making deals, making other people money, enriching stockholders, extraordinary performance. These tippees earn their tips for the same reasons that all tippees do: good job performance. And these tippees hire other tippers and other tippees.

The president of a business who gets a year-end tip, or performance bonus, is also the person ultimately responsible for hiring, firing, promoting, compensating, and paying the people who work in the organization.

In his teens, the president of a 140-person uniform rental company variously worked as a paperboy, a lawn mower, and a caddy. He was a caddy at a wannabe exclusive country club filled with striving young and old executives and their families. He remembers one incident when he was sixteen. There was a golf tournament and he was randomly assigned to carry a bag for one of the players. The player was about thirty-five years old (which to a sixteen-year-old is someone as ancient as teachers, coaches, police, other adults). It was a hot, muggy day. The golf bag was heavy. The tournament was thirty-six holes in one day. There were no written rules on what to pay a caddy. The general rule of thumb was twenty dollars for eighteen holes. Lots of golfers gave their caddies at least twenty-five dollars. For tournament play, caddies could earn fifty dollars for a single round. A good caddy could make two hundred dollars or more for a thirty-six-hole tournament.

The golfer was not a nice guy. He was rude to his teenage caddy. The golfer blamed the kid when he missed a shot: "You moved," "You made a noise," "Your shadow distracted me." He criticized the kid for not finding a few lost balls. When the game was finished, the golfer commanded his caddy, "Go clean my clubs. See if you can do that!" Ten minutes later the golfer inspected his clubs. "You call these clean? They don't match my standards for cleanliness." He gave the kid thirty dollars and walked away.

Twenty years later the one-time caddy was interviewing people to fill an important job in his company. He needed a new vice president of operations; someone to manage the pickup of uniforms, their cleaning, and redelivery to customers.

Although the job paid well, it was difficult to find someone with the required level of experience, and the special people skills to manage eighty workers, all of whom were immigrants. One guy looked perfect on paper. He met all the hiring criteria. He was highly recommended by the management recruiter.

The candidate looked familiar to the caddy. The one-time caddy, paperboy, and lawn boy studied the candidate as the potential VP described his credentials.

"Do you play golf?"

"Yes, I do."

"What would be some of your expectations of the folks who work here?" asked the caddy.

"I have very high standards for cleanliness, and each worker has to meet those standards, or else."

"Or else what?" asked the caddy.

"Or else their pay will be docked . . . for starters. That's how slackers learn . . . when it hits their pocketbook. It is part of my management philosophy," said the candidate.

"I know," said the caddy.

When told that the perfect-on-paper candidate was not acceptable, the management recruiter asked why. "Tell him," said the caddy, "that when our plant is steaming hot from the washers, dryers, and humid summer golf weather, that on those days, after carrying heavy laundry bags for ten hours, the equivalent of carrying a golf bag for thirty-six holes, we won't be able to match his standards for cleanliness."

Everyone is a tipper. Tip as if you were the tippee. Yesterday's tippee might be tomorrow's tipper.

XVI

The Most Important Question
in Business

The purpose of a business is to profitably get and keep customers. Without customers, there is no business. To get and keep customers you must be able to answer this question: "If I, the salesperson, the marketer, the manufacturer, the investor; if I were the customer, why would I do business with me?" Knowing the customer, knowing the marketplace, knowing the competition, and knowing yourself, if you were the customer, why would you do business or buy from yourself? This is the most important question in business.

You must be able to answer the question

honestly, objectively, factually. It is best if you can articulate the answer using dollarized values. For example, "If I were the customer I would do business with me because my services can save the customer $300,000 in unnecessary packaging costs." When you know the answer to this question you have a bedrock basis for pricing, advertising, selling, negotiating, doing business.

It is not easy to answer this simple question. The answer requires knowing who the customer is, which is not always apparent. The answer requires a sharp understanding of your customer's profile; his or her concerns; ability to pay; commitments to other methods; tolerance of risk; cultural barriers; mind-sets; confusions. The answer requires an accurate knowledge of the economic and "feel good" values your customer will get after investing in your product.

The answer is the blueprint for product innovation, for advertising headlines, for market segmentation, for manufacturing and distribution strategy. The answer is the blueprint for allocating investment, for hiring the right people, for se-lecting the best locations.

If you were the customer, and you can state in ten words or less why you would buy from your-self, maybe the customer will listen to you.

• XVII •

No "Bad ROT"

*B*ad ROT is bad return on time. Return is the money you make on the time you invest. Bad ROT is when a company makes a bad acquisition and diverts top talent to try to make a bad deal good. Bad ROT is calling on a customer who will never buy, or on a customer who can't change, can't make a decision, or on a customer who will never generate the revenues to justify the sales time invested. Bad ROT is trying to turn a low-potential employee into a high performer. Bad ROT is doing administration minutiae instead of working to get and keep customers. Bad ROT is squandering time solving minor problems, even irritating minor problems, that should be spent on opportunities. Bad ROT is spending hours on the phone with a credit card company to correct a five-dollar overbilling. Bad ROT is getting angry over a slight, an insult, a snotty government worker. Before you go to war with the slighter, ask yourself, and answer, "What is my gain if I win? What do I lose if I laugh off the issue and move on?" Meetings are often Bad ROT. Unless you can pinpoint how a meeting will help you and your company increase revenues, cut costs, get customers, keep customers, or accelerate innovation, the meeting is usually Bad ROT.

You want Good ROT. You want big returns on that commodity called time. So fish where the big fish are; work with your superstars; solve money-losing problems; pour the coals to every winning product, and every winning person.

Good ROT rocks. Bad ROT rots.

See Your Company Through the Salesperson's Eyes

Your company has a sales force. Maybe that sales force is one person, the owner, or senior partner, or someone else. Maybe that sales force is a 25,000-person army selling across the globe. Whatever your sales force, it does exist. And whatever your job, your background, your education, you must be able to see your company as the salesperson sees it. You need not have the same opinions or interpretations as do the salespeople, but you must see through their eyes. To not see what they see is to blind yourself to your marketplace.

Be they reps, waitresses, store clerks, counter people, owners, partners, street hawkers, customer service reps: If they sell, then they are sales-people. If they sell, then they are on the front line. They are the folks dealing directly with customers. They are the people making the sale, keeping the customer, getting rejected. These are the people who face the disinterested customer, the angry customer, the demanding customer, the critically important customer, the overbilled customer, the ever-late-paying customer, the referring customer, the shoplifter, the grateful customer. These are the sellers who have to explain higher prices, late deliveries, spotty quality, "Some assembly required," "Personal checks not accepted."

It is the salespeople who handle customer complaints, answer customer questions, satisfy the wants. It is the sales force, the front-line troops, who shake hands with customers. It is the front-line troops who wave the company flag, sing the company song, and march—often undertrained—into the inchoate marketplace.

It is the salesperson who first experiences a change in tactics; has the competitors' ads and coupons waved in his or her face; first sees new test market products show up on the shelves. It is the front-line troops who simultaneously see what the customers, the competitors, the environment, and their generals are all doing. It is the salesperson who sees how his company acts and responds and how the customer counterresponds. No one knows better than the salesperson how effective is his or her company's advertising, the quality of sales leads, manufacturing, technical service, training, innovativeness, human resources department, toll-free phone system, reputation, management. It is the salespeople—regardless of title—who have the job of explaining moronic company policies to paying customers.

The astute salesperson knows what is working and not working, what is getting and keeping customers, and what is not. The sales force is the company's eyes to the marketplace. Be those eyes shortsighted, myopic, colorblind is not a reason to ignore what those eyes see.

Not every good salesperson should run a company, or even be in top management. But everyone in top management must earn some battle ribbons in the selling war. Everyone must have sales experience. Everyone in the organization must see their job through the salesman's eyes. (The person collecting late payments must see that late-paying customer *first* through the salesman's eyes, and second, according to the payment policy book.) If you need or want credibility with the sales force you must spend time in the trenches. Everyone in management—and that includes the chief financial officer, the vice president of manufacturing, and the R&D project manager—must look through the salesperson's eyes and see the customer.

See your company, your customers, your policies, your products, your prices through the salesperson's eyes and you will see the light.

• XIX •

Child Labor
Is Good

*E*very kid should work. And the earlier the kid starts working, the earlier the kid starts to learn what he or she will need to know to be successful. Child labor is invaluable experience for future adult workers, corporate managers, and entrepreneurs. Good child labor includes working in the family business. Good child labor includes milking cows on the family farm, shoveling the neighbor's sidewalk, and delivering newspapers. Perfectly acceptable child labor is to polish fruit for the family grocery store. Perfectly acceptable child labor is to wash dishes and peel potatoes and empty the trash in Dad's diner.

Child labor should be safe. Child labor should

be paid. Child work should not replace school-work. But child labor should be.

When interviewing potential employees, if the candidates are roughly equal, hire the person who worked as a kid. Hire the paperboy or the potato picker. Hire the caddy over the country clubber. Hire the babysitter over the band member, or strike it employee-rich with a babysitter who also banged the drums smartly.

All work and no play make Jack a dull boy, but no work and all play keep Jack a boy.

· XX ·

Teach Your Girls
to Whistle

*L*ittle boys, big boys, and adults are always impressed when a little girl or woman puts her fingers in her mouth and shrieks a wolflike whistle so loud it pierces the din and attracts even the deafest of taxi drivers. Everyone marvels when a girl's whistle can be heard from one end of the soccer field to another. This is particularly true for boys between the age of six and sixty.

Attention-getting whistles have always been a male province. Men are the ones who whistle at games, at players, to get attention, to hail a cab. Not all boys and men can whistle, but their prevailing mind-set is that men can whistle and girls can't.

When a girl whistles, the girl-boy dynamics change. The girl whistler immediately gets respect. The girl whistler is no longer a pushover. The girl whistler is still a girl, but she is now different from other girls. The girl whistler is "one of the boys."

Teaching your girls to whistle teaches them it is okay to be different, to be unconventional. Teaching your girls when to whistle teaches them independence and self-reliance. Teaching a girl to whistle teaches confidence.

A girl who can whistle is unique. A girl who will whistle is confident, a winner. And whistling is a necessity at a rock 'n' roll concert.

If you can't teach your girls how to whistle, find someone who can. And pay attention to the lessons.

· XXI ·

No "They," "He,"
"She," "Her," "Him"

*I*f you are talking about more than one person,
don't use pronouns; use the persons' names.
If you are talking about two women and you refer
to one as "her," your listener or listeners will not
know whom you mean. In this busy world it is
hard to keep anyone's attention about anything.
You make it harder for people to understand you
when you are not clear, not precise. Names are
precise. Pronouns are not.

You would not put "Us" on the sign in front
of your company. You would put the company's
name on the sign. You would not replace your name
on your business card with "Me."

Using names improves communication. Using

names saves the talker's time. Talkers don't have to stop and answer the "who're they" question. Using names makes it easier for listeners to absorb and process what is being said.

Pronouns leave your audience wondering . . . if they care enough to wonder.

· XXII ·

Buzzsaw the
Buzzwords

Don't use buzzwords. Don't speak or write bafflegab. Don't say or write "gravitas." Don't use "re-engineer," "insourcing," "quantum leap," "synergy," or any of the dump-truck load of such "on message" "off message" words. Ban them all. Banish them from your vocabulary. Using the buzzwords of the day marks you as a follower, as unoriginal. Buzzwording is a herd trait. (To illustrate, there are over 100,000 companies that claim "we add value," and millions of pieces of corporate literature make claims to "value added.") Using buzzwords is a superficial communication shortcut and reflects impoverished thinking. Addicted buzzworders are lazy thinkers.

Customers are confused by buzzwords. Customers hear different companies selling different products while using the same buzzwords. Such customers don't understand the distinctions between two competitors each claiming they "add value." Thousands of companies equally claim they provide "solutions" with a "suite of products." Solutions? Duh-uh! Why would any company buy a product if it were not a solution to a problem?

Buzzwords often sound pretentious. Pompous. After all, how sick is everyone of "paradigm shift"? And what, pray tell, does paradigm mean? And who cares? Despite Yogi Berra's terse advice, no one will "look it up." If you want your readers or listeners to struggle with big words, tell them to read William Faulkner novels.

Don't use business buzzwords. Rather, invent them. You invent the next "Peter Principle," "catch-22," "tipping point." It's easy to innovate business buzzwords. Just think "outside the box." You know how to so think: like Jack does when he jumps out of his box. Think outside your sandbox, hat box, shoe box, lock box, band box, cereal box. Hurry now! Think outside the box!

And, as much as possible, ditché the cliché. Clichés are the refuge for masters of vaguery and nuance. (Suffocating clichés include "our people make the difference," "end of the day," "when the dust settles.") In addition, junk the jargon. Junk your jargon when communicating to people, such as customers, who are not in your organization. "Cut and paste" means one thing in computerese, but something different to an artist, to a tile layer, or to an elementary school teacher.

Don't buzzword. Speak and write in plain English. Be natural. Be clear. Be friendly. Your customers are being assaulted by lots of buzzworders, so if you communicate in normal language, you will have an advantage.

No dashboarding or globalizing or empowering or deep data diving. Start the saw!

Buzz-z-z-z!

• XXIII •

"Ask Mikey"

Mikey works at a car wash. Mikey doesn't know how to read. Mikey doesn't know how old he is. Mikey doesn't know the name of the town where he was born. But Mikey does know how to work. Mikey has brushed and scrubbed over one million cars. Mikey never misses a day of work, be it 101 degrees in August, or 10 degrees below zero in February. And Mikey knows if others can also work. He knows if others can or cannot do the tough, tough physical job of washing 100 to 1,000 cars a day, every day. Mikey knows if someone is going to make it, will become a good employee, or will quit and vanish. Somehow Mikey knows.

Hiring and keeping good people is kcy to a successful business. The unplanned loss of a good employee is a big cost to any business. Hiring an unsuited employee is a big cost to any business. The insidious costs of unplanned turnover and bad hires include "help wanted" advertising, interviewing, testing, background checks, training, squandered wages, legal fees, recruitment fees, workmen's compensation claims, low workplace morale, mis-spent management time, and lost revenues.

The car wash owners calculated that each mis-hire cost their company at least $1,000. The car wash owners tried all kinds of techniques to determine if a potential worker would make it or not. They gave careful interviews, checked references, checked backgrounds, talked to past employers, did police checks, gave tests. Nothing really worked. There was no predictable way to judge a prospective worker. Slouchers and slackers slipped through. Each failed hire sucked another $1,000 out of the company.

Then the owners discovered Mikey's gift. Now the owners just ask Mikey.

The new hiring process is simple. Potential employees are interviewed and background-checked. The job of washing cars is carefully explained— no embellishment, no surprise. Then the prospect is offered a one-hour preemployment paid work trial. The person can work with Mikey for one hour. Those who decline the trial are not hired. Those who take the trial are evaluated . . . by Mikey.

At the end of the trial hour, the car wash manager asks Mikey. If Mikey nods his head yes, the person is hired. If Mikey shakes his head no, the person is not hired, and the car wash saves $1,000.

Whether it is help in hiring or training or new product development or advertising or good new ideas or how to make the factory more efficient, every good company has at least one Mikey, usually many more.

If you want to improve your company, ask Mikey.

The S. W. Rule

*J*ust as great athletes miss a shot, miss a goal, make a mistake, so, too, do rainmakers, and great deal makers commonly miss making the sale. Athletes and rainmakers know they will not make every shot, make every sale. They know this reality before they enter the game. Every merchant knows that not every customer who walks through the door will buy something. Merchants know this reality before they open their doors. These players all know that failure is a reality. And they know they will undoubtedly fail much more often than succeed. They hate this reality, but they accept it. They are disappointed by every lost sale, every lost opportunity, but they know that's the way it is.

Rainmakers and winners know that a one-dollar sale is worth more than a million zeros. Rainmakers know that one yes is worth more than a hundred nos. One yes relegates all nos to the "who cares, so what" trash barrel. Rainmakers know that when they ask for the sale, open their doors, display their goods, window their menus, that some customers will say yes and will buy, and some customers will not.

Rainmakers keep selling, keep asking, because when it comes to customers, they know the truth of the S.W. Rule: "Some will. Some won't. So what?"

· XXV ·

No Slow No

*I*f you don't want to do something, or can't do something, or won't do it, then tell the guy no. Say, "Thanks, I'm flattered to be asked, but I just can't help you . . . can't participate . . . buy . . . lend . . . go along . . . do it." Always be polite. Be candid, direct, explicit. And be fast. If you know you are not going to do it, then say so right away. Don't leave the salesperson, relative, friend, fan, associate, voter hanging. Don't cause the asker to waste her time, her money, her other opportunities because you left the impression you might say yes.

The legitimate asker will not be offended. He

or she may be disappointed, wounded, depressed, flummoxed, questioning. Rejected askers can experience all kinds of emotions, but if treated well, they will deal with no. They will understand. The asker should be thankful. The asker is no longer depending on you.

Saying no as early in the process as possible sets the asker free. Now the asker can pursue other opportunities, other ways to get it done. Now the asker can rethink his request, reconsider how he asks, better articulate his sales story, or sob story, or whatever.

If the asker is disappointed after quickly learning you are not interested in the proposition, imagine how upset she will be if you wait weeks before you finally drop the "no way" chop. After such an unnecessary wait, the asker should be angry: You led her on, put her closer to a deadline, fettered her from finding other solutions, put much in jeopardy.

The longer you wait to say no, after you have decided to say no, builds your angst, your tension.

Get it over. Say no. Then the asker and you can get on with things.

The asker may abide by the S.W. Rule (see Chapter XXIV). When you say no, you will fall into the "Some won't" group. If so, "So what?"

"Miss These Shots and We Lose the Game"

The gym was packed with screaming fans. Every kid in the high school was at the game. So, too, were friends, parents, teachers, media people. This was the big game; it was for the league basketball championship. The boys on the home team had played together for years, knew one another well, and were good friends. Most of the boys were good students. All of them had fun and each had a sense of humor.

The home team was losing fifty to forty-nine when Dickie Farrell was fouled. There were two seconds left in the game. As Dickie prepared to go to the foul line, the coach caught the attention of the team captain and wildly waved him to the sideline.

"Go relax Dickie," the coach told the captain. "How am I supposed to do that?" thought the captain as he gave the coach an "Are you for real?" frown. "He's nervous, give him confidence," ordered the coach.

Dickie was at the foul line waiting for the ref to toss him the ball. He was shuffling his feet. He was rubbing the sides of his shorts. The crowd was quieting, trying not to distract Dickie. The team captain trotted over to Dickie.

"Coach wants me to relax you," said the captain.

"Great," grunted Dickie.

"Yup. You miss these two shots and we lose the game," said the captain with a fleeting, mischievous little grin. The captain slapped Dickie on the butt and ran back to his position.

Dickie almost laughed. Almost. Dickie made both free throws and the home team won the league. The crowd went wild.

In the locker room all the boys were laughing and high-fiving. They all thought it was hilarious that the coach wanted the captain to calm down Dickie Farrell. With the coach safely hidden in his office, the players imitated the coach, the captain,

Dickie, each adding, embellishing, improvising new pieces of advice, each one-upping the other. The captain's off-beat advice became high school legend. Whenever a student had to make a speech, play solo in the band, recite lines in a play, act in the talent show, or make a crucial play in a crucial game, someone would invariably suggest, "Miss these shots and we lose the game."

Later, grilled by his coach, the captain explained: "My grandfather says that humor often makes the toughest situations more tolerable. My grandfather says that soldiers and cops and effective politicians and good businessmen ease tension with humor."

"And you thought what you said was funny?" asked the incredulous coach.

"Very," said the captain.

"I don't get it," said the coach.

"Yeah, I know," said the captain.

Twenty years later the team captain was running a big division of a big company. His coworkers considered him to be fun, funny, witty, and a winner.

Still a winner.

· XXVII ·

Customers Don't Like Your Politics

*I*f you do business in a public place, don't use your place of business to publicize your politics, your political party, your burning causes. Your place of business is for business; it's not a political campaign headquarters. A lifelong Democrat may not want to do business at a place where Republican banners are waving in the breeze, and vice versa. It's hard to get and keep good customers without unnecessarily offending them. So don't offend them.

Customers vote with their money. Telling one customer to "vote for X" is telling another customer to "vote your money at my competitor." Heed the mannerly admonishment of your parents: "It is impolite to discuss politics and religion in social settings." Thus it follows that unless your store or company is a Bible store, or only sells religious products of any faith, don't punch your customers in the face with your religious beliefs. Your place of business is not a church (unless, of course, you are a pastor, rabbi, minister); it is not hallowed ground. It is a business. Atheists and agnostics must be as welcome as future saints. If, for religious or other beliefs, you choose not to sell certain legal products, or you choose to close on special days or times, that is an anti-customer, anti-business choice.

Customers also do not like your favorite football team. Customers don't care if you adore the same sports team as do they. Customers only care about you solving their problems and fulfilling their needs in a highly satisfactory way.

Don't you or your employees wear "Vote for Dufus" buttons or "Save the Mosquito" T-shirts or "Power to the Puppets" baseball caps. Wear your company's logo, and be thrilled to serve any good customer.

Get out the vote. Support your candidate. Send money to charity and good causes. Donate time to your school. Put money in the collection basket. But don't do nonbusiness activities at your business. Nonbusiness leads to no business.

Amen!

· XXVIII ·

Don't Park in Front of Your Store

*I*n hundreds of parking-starved locales around the country, merchants, restaurateurs, dentists, real estate agents stupidly park in front of their stores and places of business. That parking space is a money space. Take away that "customer who spends money" parking space, and take away revenue. No excuses. No rationalization. Park in the back of the cemetery if necessary. If one out of one hundred people who park in that money space does business with you, you win. If one customer keeps driving because his or her money space is now a convenience space for a noncustomer, you lose.

Big companies make the same mistake. Big

companies too often reserve the most convenient spaces for self-important executives. These executives, as do the smart salespeople who call on the company, should park in the back of the building. Reserve the most convenient parking spaces for the customers who pay the executives' salaries.

The bank owned and occupied a fourteen-story building on Main Street in a bustling city. Next door to the bank, attached by a walkway, was a six-story parking garage. The parking garage was used by senior bank executives and by customers. The walkway was on the second floor of the garage. Parkers on the first floor could get to the walkway using a wide, well-lit open stairway. Anyone parking on floors three through six could get to the walkway by either using an ancient, slow, smelly elevator, or by climbing down (and later back up) a dim and dirty interior staircase. One of the reasons the elevator received scant attention and the ugly staircase received no maintenance was because no bank executive ever used, visited, or inspected the customers' entrance to the bank.

One customer, heavily courted and coveted

by the bank, was a wealthy real estate developer and investor. The developer wanted to borrow $90,000,000, and the bank wanted to make the lucrative loan and collect service fees, points, interest, and prestige. The occasion was a major go–no go meeting at the bank replete with lawyers, accountants, et al. The customer arrived early, but squandered time hunting for a parking place as he drove from the first floor to the sixth. On floor six, the uncovered rooftop floor, there were some open spaces. It was pouring rain. The customer slogged through the rain and puddles to the elevator door, where a ragged sign read, "Temporarily out of order, use stairs." The trip down four flights of stairs was interesting . . . if you were an urban anthropologist. From the bottles and trash and graffiti, one could learn the wine of choice of local winos, what brand of cigarettes was in vogue, and how various gang members memorialized themselves.

Shaking hands with the important customer, the bank president said, "It's really raining hard today. You should have parked in the bank's garage."

"Hmmm," thought the customer, "this guy is an idiot."

The meeting was going well. The customer figured an idiot's money was just as good as anyone's. "There is one other point," said the bank president, "and this is good news for you. The bank has a number of excellent real estate professionals on staff. They are skilled in the design and marketing of the kind of upscale condominiums and retail space that you will be building. And with a loan this size it is bank policy that at least one of our people be part of the approval process on certain phases of the project."

"Approval process?" prompted the customer.

"Yes. That's right. The bank believes it can both protect its money and help you succeed by lending—pardon the [chuckle, chuckle] pun—by lending its expertise on project design, unit pricing, and retail tenant approval."

"I have a question," said the customer. "If someone were interested in buying a five-hundred-thousand-dollar condominium, when do you think their buying experience would begin: in the condo itself; in the building lobby; in the parking area; reading our ads?"

"Well," answered the bank president, "since no one believes advertising anyway, I guess it would be when they drive in. So, what do you say? Are we going to be putting up that building?"

"Walk me to my car," said the customer. "We can talk more about the customer buying experience, and you will have my answer."

The bank is no longer in business. The real estate developer is doing well.

Let the customer park in the president's space. Let the customer park as close to your cash register as possible. You park in the rain. Be a rainmaker.

· XXIX ·

Don't Put Anything on Your Store Windows

*I*f you owned a store or restaurant or fitness center, and you had a choice to face your customers with big, clean, clear windows, or a solid brick wall covered with graffiti and weather-tattered posters and signs . . . which would you choose? If you had a chance to run a full-page ad, would you advertise your business, your products, your brand; or would you spend your company's money to promote the local high school fund-raiser, or ten different credit card companies? The question should be rhetorical, yet millions of businesses clutter their windows, their ads, their trucks, their catalogs, their business cards with stuff that blurs communication to customers.

Windows are for window-shopping. Walking through your doors is the first customer action that precedes a sale. Why deface your stores and windows with, for example, credit card stickers and news of community events? Customers expect businesses to accept all credit cards. Turning your doors into a credit card collage is unnecessary, irrelevant. Your windows are not bulletin boards. They are a place to display merchandise, to entertain customers, to attract customers. If you feel the need to display the ads and flyers announcing the Lions Club pancake breakfast, pin them to a bulletin board in the back of your store. Interested customers will have to walk by your merchandise to read the notices. Take a lesson from the master merchants of Fifth Avenue in New York City. Their holiday window displays make the stores a destination, generate publicity, and enhance the shopping experience.

Everything you do to talk to the customer should be crisp, clear, simple. One message in an ad, not one hundred. Trucks that are covered with telephone numbers and addresses and multiple messages and "How's my driving?" say nothing. Business cards with a string of MBA, CLU, PhD, FDAC are self-serving and bewildering.

Windows, not walls. Billboards, not bulletin boards. Message, not mess. Clarity, not clutter.

Stop Eating
So Much!

*T*he executive had gained forty pounds. The weight gain bothered the executive and he wanted to lose the lard. One evening, on the road, the executive happened to be dining in a place where an internationally known physical fitness guru was also dining. Coincidentally, the executive's boss had a longtime friendship with the guru. Figuring his boss's friendship was an entrée to introduce himself, the overweight executive did exactly that.

"Mr. Fitness Guru," said the exec, "my name is George McCardiac. I work for Liam O'Flaherty. Liam says you guys are old friends."

The guru said, "If you work for Liam you

must be a good guy. Thank you for saying hello."

"I don't want to intrude," said the executive, "but maybe you can help me. I've recently gained a lot of weight. You're the world's greatest expert on getting and staying in shape. Can you recommend a diet or an exercise regimen or one of those pills they sell on television? I need to do something."

The fitness guru looked at the guy. "I work with businesspeople all over the world to improve physical and mental health. My company provides daily and weekly workout plans. We sell equipment, nutrients, diet advice, and supplements. For some CEOs we charge ten thousand dollars for a one-day evaluation and personalized better health plan. But because you work with Liam, I'll give you the big secret, and give it to you for free. Come closer."

The fat executive leaned in to learn the secret of weight loss. The guru whispered, "Stop eating so damn much! Nice meeting you, George."

Your brain makes you money. Your body carries your brain. Take care of your body.

• XXXI •

Always Cut Your Meat into Dime-Sized Pieces

You are having dinner with an important customer or investor or person of importance. Suddenly, you feel yourself unable to breathe, panicked, paralyzed, pointing to your throat, going down for the last count. Then the strong hands of an alert waitress crunch your chest and you launch a rib-eye chunk into your customer's salad plate. You are alive, which is good, but the deal may be dead, which is not good. If the deal were to die, know that the demise was preventable.

You can prevent potential embarrassment, prevent killing a deal, ruining a dinner for everyone else, and your death by cutting your filet mignon into dime-sized bites. Dime-sized bites rarely choke you to death. Large pieces of food might lodge in your throat, and if not dislodged, will indeed kill your sale. (Choking is the fourth most common cause of unintentional injury mortality in the United States.)

Other than self-inflicted death, there are other good business reasons to cut your steak into dime-sized pieces. Smaller pieces cause you to eat slower. This gives you time to listen to your customer and partners and associates. Listening leads to increased sales. Eating slower is better table etiquette than gobbling. Eating slower reduces the chances of spilling food on your blouse. Eating slower leads to faster sales, faster career promotions.

If a waitress ever Heimlichs you out of heaven, tip her with exuberance. And thank God for making waitresses.

You can't get to the top if you are six feet under. Cut your meat into dime-sized pieces. You will live to make a dollar.

· XXXII ·

Never Overserve Yourself

Overserving is drinking too many alcoholic beverages at one time. (Scarfing down two double cheeseburgers for lunch is another form of overserving, but not the business killer as is pounding down two double martinis.) Never get intoxicated in front of customers or business associates of any kind. This is not a moral or religious-based rule: It is business. If you over-serve yourself, you will lose your edge. You will lose some of your authority. You will show vul-nerability, weakness, and lack of control. If you get intoxicated, you will make a mistake, miss a clue, miss a cue, blow an opportunity. Even to the hardest-drinking customer on the planet, you will be diminished and reduced. And imagine the impression you would make on a nondrinker. You may become, as the gossipers say, "a topic of conversation."

You don't want to commit any unforced errors. You don't want anybody to have any photos, anything on you. Your customers want you to be a rock, a pro, totally dependable, ever alert. Your customers do not want to see you sloshed. Your customers do not want to hear about your barroom indulgences. If, perchance, you accidentally overserve yourself, never mention it. Never boast about "getting hammered," closing the bar, or drinking someone under the table. That is high school.

It is infinitely better to be a stone-cold seller than a stoned-out heller.

Save your partying for your sorority reunion or annual rugby team dinner. They might understand.

The "What, Why, and How"
Rule

A key to success and advancement in an organization is to get propelled up the ladder by dynamic, achieving, high performance underlings (or subordinates or employees or associates or team members or whatever you call those good folks lower on the chain of command). The first factor in the success formula is to hire smart people with good attitudes. Then teach and train continuously. Your job is to tell your superstars what needs to be done, and why the what needs to be done. Leave the how, the doing of the job, up to them. Inspect progress now and then. If the job is off track, make considerate suggestions. Give lots of praise. Bestow all the credit.

And keep your hands raised to grab the next rung.

• XXXIV •

Don't Be Phony

*B*eing phony, being something you are naturally not, is a type of dishonesty. Being phony is affecting an accent, putting on "airs" (as your grandmother might have said), faking an expertise. Phonies give false compliments. Phonies pad résumés, ask insincere questions, and double-talk.

People spot phonies in a heartbeat. Customers are repelled by the slick, the glib, the superficial. Coworkers see likable phonies as insecure. Coworkers see unlikable phonies as untrustworthy. Potential partners shrink from the counterfeit. Radio listeners cringe when one cohost constantly fake-laughs at the other host's unclever repartee. Radio listeners gag when the news commentator, speaking in unaccented, perfect English, interjects a French or Spanish or Italian phrase or name or place, and does so in an elaborate, distinct, grand French or Italian or Spanish pronunciation. Even friends groan internally when the traveler cops an accent to describe the first-time visit to "Firenze in Toscana in Italia," which is what Italians call what Americans call Florence, Tuscany, Italy. Using a vast vocabulary is fine if that's you. It is fine to use unusual words if that is how you commonly speak. But using the arcane and exotic to impress, and not to express, is phony. If quoting passages of poetry in public is your thing, then do Walt Whitman proud. But spending two hours in the language lab so that you pompously ape Henry V's St. Crispin Day speech is an act. And since no table wine is made with hints of chocolate, eucalyptus, raspberry, plums, melon, licorice, honeysuckle, or anything but grapes, refrain from such fictions when describing the brawny cabernet or perky little pinot. And since good table wines are never smoky, woody, corky, rusty, musty, crusty, or dusty, let's give that farce the hook.

Lifting the glass, he marveled at the ruby-red tints glistening with promise: "Ah, such a wine. It has all the exuberance of Chaucer, without the concomitant crudités!"

"So-oh fun!"

Yup. And so-oh faux.

Be real. Being real leads to real deals.

XXXV

Don't Shirk

"Shirk" means to avoid doing what has to be done, or to avoid taking responsibility. Shirk means hiding, evading, running from the battle. (Procrastination is mild shirking. Procrastination is putting off what you ultimately will do; shirking is not doing.)

Shirk means not confronting what must be confronted. Shirkers let coworkers down. Shirkers put the company in jeopardy. Shirkers are never picked for the A-team. Shirkers are the first to be fired, the last to be hired. Shirkers are afraid. Shirkers are lazy. Hire workers, not shirkers.

Don't shirk. Do the messy, dirty, embarrassing deed. Visit the irate customer. Call the supplier you haven't paid in ninety days. If you made a mistake, call, explain, and offer some remedies.

If you forgot, or didn't give your friends a wedding gift, send one today, even if you are two years late. If you didn't send a timely thank-you note, send it, then call. Schedule your physical. Get a colonoscopy. Get your teeth cleaned.

Unsheath thy mighty sword and sally forth into the fray.

XXXVI

How to Make
a Decision

Determine if the outcome of the decision is somewhat revocable, or irrevocable. If the outcome is revocable, changeable, not permanent, then decide.

Determine exactly how much time you have before you must make the decision. Whether you have 100 days or 100 seconds, use 90 percent of that time thinking, considering. Do not squander one second fretting, anguishing, panicking, choking.

Determine, as best possible, the financial cost of the consequence of being wrong. Determine the cost of doing nothing. Determine the potential gain of being right. Numbers clarify.

Using whatever scheme and objective rigor available, determine a probability percentage as to the chances of being wrong and being right. Shuffle, tango, balance the probability percentages against the financial costs and gains.

Make a list of all the possible "unintended consequences" of each decision option. Quantify the consequences. Estimate the probability of occurrence. This calculation is crucial in making big decisions. If it is a big decision that goes badly, no one wants to hear the all-too-common "unintentional consequences" excuse (see Chapter XLIX).

In addition to thinking about what might happen the day after your decision, think about the "day" after the day after. (These are metaphorical days, of course; somewhat like those in the Old Testament. It took God six "days" to create everything, and on the seventh "day" he took a well-deserved break. Those days, it is safe to surmise, were slightly longer than the twenty-four-hour variety.)

Determine what facts you must know before deciding, and keep gathering those facts, and thinking and planning, up to the moment you must decide. One axiom of decision making is that you will never have all the facts. Incomplete data is not an excuse for dithering.

After making the decision, do not second-guess yourself. And don't be swayed by those who think you are right, or by those who think you are wrong. Be swayed by the facts. But don't get cemented into your decision. If new facts, new imperatives emerge, you must honestly, objectively, hardheadedly rethink, reconsider. Only a fool stays with a decision when *new* facts signal a better way.

· XXXVII ·

How to Listen . . .
for the Sounds of Money

*E*very marriage counselor touts the value of listening. Good psychiatrists make a good living by good listening. Every politician learns to dazzle and enthrall by earnestly nodding while intently peering into the talker's eyes. Every selling manual on the planet exhorts salespeople to listen. There are a million books and courses on "active listening," "understanding verbal clues," "reading body language." Oodles of professional speakers highlight the importance of listening with over-told and ancient old clichés such as, "God gave us two ears, but one mouth," and "The customer can't say yes when you are talking." So with all the talk about listening, why is this critical success skill so rare?

Just as every golfer knows the importance of hitting a golf ball straight, and knows the importance of making a seven-foot putt, it's the *how* to properly swing and hit the ball that eludes. People know the importance of listening, they just don't know how.

The secret to moneymaking listening is to listen *for* something. You must listen for what you need to know to make the sale, cut the deal, achieve your business objective. Specifically, you must listen for numbers, facts, dates, names. If a customer tells you he wants a "longer lasting" device, you must ask, "What do you mean by longer lasting?" If the customer answers, "A device I can use for a few years," you have heard nothing. You must ask, "What do you mean by a few years?" If the customer answers, "Three years," then you have a number. You have correctly listened.

Imagine the boss sending one guy into the forest (on a sales call) and telling him to listen. The boss sends a second person into the forest, telling her to listen for the sound of a certain songbird, or a falling branch. When both emerge from the forest, which person is more likely to have heard the songbird? Imagine the same two people being sent onto the streets of New York City. One is told to listen, and one is told to listen *for* someone speaking a foreign language. Which person is more likely to come back with a list of twenty people speaking twenty foreign languages?

To listen, you must listen *for* something.

To be able to hear what you need to hear, you must first determine what numbers, facts, dates, names you need to know to make the sale, to do the deal. You must make this determination while precall-planning your meeting. For example, you may determine that to safely buy an olive tree farm, you need to know the selling price of olives over the last few years, who the most reputable olive buyers are, and when the harvest must be completed. Before the deal-making meeting, craft and write out the questions you must ask that will encourage the person(s) you meet to give you the selling price per ton of olives over the last four years, the names of people with whom to do business, critical harvest dates, and so on.

Ask the preplanned questions, and keep asking, until you hear the numbers, facts, dates, and names. Take notes. Be on high receive. When you hear numbers, write them down. That's how to listen.

Keep listening until you hear ka-ching.

· XXXVIII ·

Don't Teach the
Quarterback to Catch

A standard question in job interviews is "What is your biggest weakness?" This is a dumb question. When the job candidate answers, "I can't dance the Pablo salsa, but I can sell," does the hiring manager make a note saying, "Needs work on his tango"? A standard part of performance reviews is to "balance" the employee's strengths and weaknesses. "You did an excellent job creating and introducing ten new products worth millions in new revenues, but [there is always a but!] you don't get your expense accounts in on time, your monthly reports are bare bones at best, and you let anyone park in your company-assigned parking space."

Working on fixing weaknesses is a waste of time. Working on strengths is where the money is. If you are good at something, if your associates are good at something, work to make that something even better. Whatever you do that gives you an edge in the marketplace; whatever you produce for which customers are willing to pay; whatever works is where you work.

Assume you owned an American football team and you paid big money to acquire a quarterback who was a terrific passer, and an end who could catch anything. Suppose the quarterback could not catch and the end could not pass. Would you have your coaches work to improve the quarterback's catching? Or would you have the quarterback work on passing in the rain, on sideline passes, on better accuracy? Would you have the end practice catching a wet football, making sideline catches, or throwing a spiral?

Weaknesses are too often seen as problems to solve. Many managers believe they exist to solve problems, thus they work on weaknesses. So helping the brilliant but brusque engineer better "relate" to her associates is a typical management diversion. Forget about it. If she can't relate, but she can invent and design, hide her someplace where she can pound out inventions and designs.

Lodovico Buonarroti Simoni was a nasty, unlikable brute who had the distinctly unsociable habit of poor personal hygiene. He yelled and he smelled. But the boy could wield a wicked chisel and wave a wild paintbrush. When the Vatican's top moneyman, the exchequer, complained that Michelangelo was a financial disaster, that he was over budget, that he routinely tossed receipts, that he charged stuff at local merchants without approval, and that he gulped *vino rosso* like it was *acqua minerale,* Pope Julius II sighed and answered the cardinal, "Get Mike a hundred more of the best chisels, and a hundred more of the best paintbrushes the guilds can make. Throw in a case of Brunello di Montepulciano. And tell him whenever he's finally done with the ceiling, I need two more Pietàs. One more thing, Excellency: I want Mike painting. I don't want him wasting a second thinking about money. You're the moneyman. You do the money. *Capisce?*"

Work on the products customers buy, no matter how old and boring. Work on the people who are proven cash register ringers, no matter how difficult to manage. Work on strengths. Work on what is working or you won't be.

Never Give the Coach
a Reason to Bench You

*T*he junior varsity game was played before the varsity game. Most of the kids on the JV team were freshmen and sophomores. Most of the kids on the varsity were juniors and seniors. Two or three of the kids on the JV would dress for the varsity game. Usually the JV kids sat at the end of the bench. Unless the varsity game was a blowout, either winning or losing, the JV players did not get into the game. Some of the JV players were as good, or almost as good, some possibly better than the varsity. But seniors always got the nod over sophomores. Every kid on the JV team would kill to start for the varsity.

During the last quarter of the JV game, the

varsity would dress for their game. On this night, after the JVs won their game and gathered in the locker room, the head coach went up to one of the good sophomore JV players and said, "Joe, I need a favor. Mick forgot his sneakers. You are the same shoe size. Let him borrow your shoes for tonight's game."

Joe looked at the coach and said, "Nope."

"What do you mean no?" demanded the coach. "Give Mick your shoes."

"Coach," said Joe. "I play guard like Mick. If he can't play, I can."

"You've never started a varsity game. This is a big game. The team needs Mick. This game is important. Shoes. Now!"

"This game is not that important to Mick. He didn't come ready to play. I did. I'm dressed. I can play. He's not getting my shoes."

"Joe, you could be kicked off the team for this. Please let Mick borrow your shoes."

"Nope. Giving up my shoes means I don't want to play. I'm not doing it."

Joe wasn't kicked off the team. The head

coach fumed that Mick forgot his shoes. He was impressed with Joe's pluck. Joe started the game and he starred. The coach owed Joe the starting position for the next game. Joe played well again. Joe started every other varsity game until he graduated. Mick rode the bench as a sub until he graduated.

It is baseball legend that in 1925 Wally Pipp, the starting first baseman for the New York Yankees, asked to sit out a game because of a headache. Pipp was replaced by a rookie named Lou Gehrig, who went on to play in 2,130 consecutive games and went into the Baseball Hall of Fame. Wally Pipp never played another minute for the Yankees.

To get to the top, to be a winner, to make big money, to win a varsity letter, to make "Employee of the Year," you must first be in the game. You must be a player, a competitor. You must be on the field, on the pitch, on the course, at the customer. If you are not in the race you can't win, place, or show. There are no checkered flags for drivers in the pits. There are no bonuses, no commissions, no career promotions, no parking place with initials for the MIA employee. Always be there when the organization needs you. Always do what is asked. Do it better than expected. Do the miserable jobs that need to be done, particularly those jobs that no one else wants to do. Do these miserable jobs with joy. Take the overseas assignment. Turn around the underperforming department or factory or region. Be the go-to gal or guy. Never be sick. Never be tired. Never half-arse it. Jump at any opportunity to shine.

Always be ready to play.

And never forget your playing shoes.

Only Hire People You Would Invite Home to Dinner

Abusiness, a company, a firm, a rock 'n' roll band, a team, a traveling circus, a Broadway cast, a criminal enterprise, a board of advisers have much in common with a family. They have similar DNA, the same chemistry, over time a oneness. The members might disagree, but they must get along. They may argue within, but they do not speak against the "family" in public. There will be quarrels and politics and jostling, but there is a commonality, a special culture, a way of thought, crises mutually survived that bind, if loosely, the members. In good organizations, good people care about and respect the opinions of their comrades. The same is true in families.

Family members care about what the other family members think. They care because they are alike, with a common set of values. The values learned in a good family are values that inform all kinds of life decisions, from picking a pet to a job to a spouse. What the family thinks is one reason why "meeting the parents" is such a big deal. ("They'll love you." "They'll hate me.") Meeting the parents is one time to ratchet up your mojo and display good manners, especially table manners. It is why the movies *Guess Who's Coming to Dinner* and *Meet the Fockers* and countless others of similar theme resonate with family members.

People like or dislike or let pass or ignore a million aspects of another person's personality, style, being. People can work with, do business with, and socialize with a person they wouldn't marry or give mouth-to-mouth resuscitation. That's okay; everybody is different. Hiring someone very different from yourself is often successful. But in the hiring process ask yourself, "Would I invite this person to dinner with my family?" If in the deepest caverns of your brain, you sense that your family would not like the person, for whatever reason, then go slowly. This is particularly true if your family is an open-arms, welcoming mob. Your family's values and concerns are yours.

Your family mirrors the kinds of customers with whom you like to do business, the people who will invest time or money in you, the bosses who value you and promote you. Your family values influence the kinds of people you judge to be good managers, good employees, good comrades, good suppliers, good partners. If you are reluctant to bring a candidate home for dinner, don't invite him, and don't hire him. Something in your value system, something in your trustworthy pool of intuition, is warning you.

If in doubt, invite the candidate and spouse, if there is one, home to dinner. After dinner, check with the family. They'll let you know.

· XLI ·

Treat Customers as Important Guests to Your Home

*I*f a celebrity you like, or a politician you support, or a dignitary from any field you respected were a guest at your home, how would you treat him or her? You would be warm, welcoming, hospitable. You would anticipate his needs, serve what he prefers. You would pay attention to what he says. You would not ignore him. You would let him use your phone, your bathrooms, your crystal goblets. You would be generous. You would not hustle him out the door. You would not say no easily or often.

Such visitors are not necessarily a customer or partner. They are guests. They do not ring the cash register or boost your career.

As you treat guests to your home, so should you treat customers, aka guests, when they visit your store, your hospital, your church, your stadium, your dealership, your place of business. Customers have choices. When customers choose you, make them never forget they made the correct choice. Make your customer feel like a fawned-over celebrity.

Some marketers and merchants do not understand this notion. They treat customers as transactions, as inconveniences, as tiresome, as hagglers, as picky-picky complainers. For example, some marketers . . .

- Have employees who don't speak the same language as does the customer.
- Have bathrooms that are off-limits, or are as filthy as a tar pit.
- Don't constantly brew fresh coffee.
- Have lobbies or waiting rooms with furniture picked up on the side of the road.
- Don't accept all credit cards.

- Close the store when customers want to shop.
- Offer six-month-old magazines that are germ factories.
- Scold the customer with "No, no" signs everywhere (such as "No shoes means no service," "No cell phones." No nothing!).
- Refuse, or balk at taking back impaired merchandise.
- Fight customers who want to drop a service, get out of a one-sided agreement.

Visit your business as would a customer. Gauge the experience as would a customer. Are you treated like a guest, or an interloper? Nothing a customer wants is a problem. A customer request is a chance to prove that he or she made the right choice in choosing to do business with you.

A customer visit promises treasure. Customer visits must be treasured.

· XLII ·

You're Not at School to Eat Your Lunch

*A*t any age, school is where you learn. School is where you learn to read, write, count, and think for yourself. School is where you make friends and learn about people. There are all kinds of schools. There is Socrates' tree, Davy Crockett's one-roomer, night school, on-the-job training, and the proverbial school of hard knocks. The family dinner table is school. So is watching a great boss in action. It matters not what kind of school. If you are not going to school to make your life better today or in the future, you are wasting time and money.

Any able-minded person too weak or too lazy to learn is irrelevant.

The late Legh Knowles, legendary chairman of Beaulieu Vineyard winery, and superstar marketer and salesman, would occasionally give a compliment of highest praise. He would say, "He didn't go to school to eat his lunch." To Legh Knowles, who dropped out of school at twelve years old, who made over 160 records with Glenn Miller, and who was self-taught, someone who "didn't go to school to eat his lunch" was smart, savvy, ambitious, going places, worth watching.

Be the person who didn't go to school to eat the lunch.

· XLIII ·

Whisper:
"Will You Marry Me?"

*T*he superstar salespeople, the rainmakers, the big moneymakers, do one thing that ordinary sellers rarely, if ever, do: They always ask for the sale, or they ask the customer for a commitment to an action that leads to a sale. The stereotype is that great salespeople are flamboyant, talkative, glib, cigar-smoking, back-slapping good old boys, good young gals. Some great salespeople are exactly that. But most great salespeople, like great leaders, are quiet, calm, questioners, listeners, note takers. Great salespeople encourage the customer to do 80 percent of the talking during a sales call. And when timely, the great salesperson will say,

"We can help you make the problem go away. Will you let us?"

Whisper: "Will you marry me?" is a reminder to ask for the business, and to do so in an appropriate manner. Future spouses, like customers, expect you to pop the question.

After "yes," you can pop the champagne.

Only Bet
on Yourself

When he was nine years old, his favorite football team was winning by thirty points with less than five minutes left in the game. Convinced of victory, he offered to bet his grandfather on the outcome of the game. His grandfather laughed and agreed. The stakes were ninety-four cents, all the money the nine-year-old had in his pocket. Five seconds after the boy and his grandfather shook hands, the losing team began one of the greatest comebacks in the history of the sport. The nine-year-old hated to lose, and handing over his ninety-four cents worsened the agony of his defeat. His grandfather told the boy, "Only bet on yourself. Don't bet on events and people you can't control or influence. Don't bet on what you don't know or don't understand."

Three years later the twelve-year-old and his father were standing by the lake where they lived. The boy's father said he could walk on water. The kid bet his father five dollars that walking on water was impossible. They shook hands to cement the bet. Three months later the boy's father walked on water and collected five bucks from a furious twelve-year-old.

"You cheated," said the boy.

"If I had offered to bet you, you would be right. But you wanted to bet. You wanted to bet because you thought it was impossible to walk on water. Not much is impossible. Next time, think it through. Only bet on yourself, on people you trust. And don't bet against yourself. Want to shake on it?" said Dad.

"I quit betting," said the kid while shaking hands, "you can bet on it."

"You can earn five bucks if you shovel the snow and clear a skating area for Mom and everybody. The lake is frozen two feet thick," said Dad.

Betting on yourself is a sure bet.

• XLV •

Sign All
the Checks

*C*ash is the bloodstream of any organization, be it a company, a college, a country, a charity, a household. Cash flow is the movement of money into and out of a business. Cash is the money in the bank after all the bills are paid. The bills are paid with checks. Checks are cash. Cash going out of a company is like a body bleeding (hence the phrase "bleeding cash"). Signing all the checks lets you take the pulse of your company's bloodstream.

If you just bought or acquired a business, signing one month's checks, and asking questions as you sign the checks, will give you a fast understanding of how the business works, how it is run, how its managers think. As you sign checks to pay suppliers, you can ask, "Who is this company? What do they do? Why did we hire them? How long have we worked with them? What is their performance record?" and a hundred other questions. You can ask questions about employees, phone services, insurance, rent, accountants, landscapers, and every other entity to whom your company sends money.

How the cash is spent is proof of the company's actual priorities. A company that spends money on research and development means that innovation and new products are a priority. How the cash is spent is a measure of how a strategy is being implemented. For example, if an organization's avowed strategy and expressed number one priority is to, say, teach elementary school students how to read, yet spends no money on books or teachers, then the check signer knows that the strategy execution is underfunded. Signing all the checks ferrets out embezzlement, identifies areas for expense control, and red alerts possible misspending.

It is easier for someone running a fifteen-person company to sign all the checks than it is for someone in charge of a 1,500-person organization. This is one reason why people running small businesses more often sign all the checks than do folks running big organizations. Another is that small organizations are closer to their cash. They hear the cash register ring. They hear when the cash register is quiet. They answer customer calls. Small-business people make change, run credit cards, total daily receipts, make deposits. Small-business people hear a tray of glasses crash, know when it rains, scramble when a delivery truck breaks down. These people see the cash come in, and see the cash rush out.

Cash is the only way to really keep score. It is the only way to measure the vitality of a company, or divisions, or parts of a company. The people who run small businesses know all about cash. Without cash they don't meet payroll.

The people who run big businesses know all about cash, but more often it is people down the ladder, closer to the customers, and closer to the suppliers, that impact the cash in and cash out.

Because he was a proven, able, excellent executive he was given the job of fixing the big problem business. His experience was primarily working in and managing well-run companies. Then overnight, he found himself running a dysfunctional 1,500-person company. The place was a madhouse. The computer systems didn't talk to each other. Reports were hopelessly late. The data were suspect. Employee turnover was rampant. Temporary employees were everywhere. Shipments to customers were dangerously late. Customers were screaming, threatening, leaving. No one knew how much cash was on hand at any one time. Without lifting a shovel the new guy noticed three different office equipment suppliers' trucks; six advertising agencies; an in-house advertising department; an in-house video production group; four hiring and recruiting firms; three travel agencies. Walking through the factory the new guy saw pallets of unshipped products, shelves of excess parts and components, bins of discarded items. Walking through customer service he heard unanswered phones ringing and ringing. Walking through R&D he saw scientists playing poker on company computers. Back in his office there were dozens of pink phone slips, from outraged customers, from outraged salespeople, bucked up to him just because he was the new guy.

The new guy had a big-league MBA. He had a proven, superlative track record. He was surrounded by a million-dollar-plus payroll of executives. Expensive consultants' reports were piled to the ceiling. But it wasn't enough. So he called his father. His father ran a successful small business that had forty-five full-time employees and a fluctuating number of seasonal workers.

"So, Dad, you got any ideas?"

"Sign all the checks," said his father.

"Personally? Like you used to do?"

"Yup."

"But, Dad, this is a billion-dollar business. There must be thousands of checks every week," said the new guy.

"Get an extra pen," said Dad.

"Sign all the checks?" moaned the new guy.

"You'll find a lot of slimy critters hiding under

the rocks. Behind the checks are the rocks," said Dad.

"Do you still sign all your company's checks?" asked the new guy.

"Every once in a while," said Dad. "And I do sign all checks over five thousand dollars. But not before I ask some questions."

"Sign all the checks?" sighed the new guy.

"Don't delay the payroll. Deal with that later. Start with the top one hundred suppliers. And probe the guys using the suppliers."

"Are you sure?" asked the new guy.

"Our computers are linked. Our deliveries are on time. Our customers love us."

"Okay, Dad. Thanks."

"Good boy. Write legibly. Call me later."

Two months later the new guy felt some calming in the madhouse. Four months later the company was a drivable machine: not well-oiled, not well-tuned, but enabled to steer and to brake. The new guy often mused that in all his business school classes, and with all his past bosses, no one had ever mentioned the power of the pen. No one, except Dad, of course. "And what else did Dad say at dinner?" the new guy thought to himself.

The first thing corporate turnaround experts do is take control of all cash conduits, and sign or review all checks. If you sign all the checks, or have them signed by a trusted confidant, your business may never need a turnaround expert.

· XLVI ·

Get Your Point Across,
but Never Be Rude

*T*here were five family members seated in the restaurant. There were three girls, ages four, nine, and eleven; one boy about thirteen; and their mother. Everyone was well-dressed and well-groomed. The girls were bright and talkative. Probably because the girls were chatterboxes, their older brother quietly read the menu. The kids were well-behaved and the girls helped one another, especially the four-year-old, in reading the menu. Even though the girls claimed they were starving, they could not make up their minds on what to order. Mom listened attentively as they asked what certain dishes were, mildly suggested they tone down the volume, and answered their questions. The waiter bustled by and Mom asked if he could bring some bread for the table. He said he would, and would do so "right away."

Time passed, and although the waiter bustled back and forth by their table, he did not bring the bread. Youthful impatience plus several hours since lunch times four equals a mini Mt. Vesuvius. As the waiter once again bustled past, the nine-year-old waved her hand and piped out, "Mr. Waiter, where's our bread?" Mom's head shot up, but she said nothing until the waiter nodded to the table, and bustled away.

In a quiet voice, when all four kids were attentive, Mom said to the nine-year-old, "You may always get your point across, but you must never be rude. You are encouraged, expected to get your point across, but you must never be rude. You made your point to the waiter, which is fine, and when he returns, you thank him for bringing the bread in your nicest voice. Okay?"

In today's maelstrom of honking horns and carping critics and pontificating pundits all making their points as if they were deranged, anyone who is independent and polite stands out among the mob.

• XLVII •

Don't Immediately Take
the First Offer

*I*f the price for something is negotiable, such
as real estate, boats, antiques, paintings, con-
tracts, then negotiate. If you are selling a building
for $200,000, and the buyer offers $180,000,
make a counter at, say, $192,000, even if you
would jump at the original offer. If you accept the
$180,000 and don't counter, the buyer will think
that he or she should have offered $170,000. This
buyer unease could lead to new deal-delaying or
deal-breaking issues later in the negotiation.

If you are the buyer for the $200,000 building
be aware that the listed price is the seller's first
offer. Even if you believe that the $200,000 price
is honest, fair, and a bargain, you should counter

at, say, $180,000. If you offer the full $200,000, the seller may feel that he or she priced the building too low, below its true value. This seller unease could lead to new terms and conditions that will complicate the negotiation.

It is human nature to want to get the best price whether selling or buying. Every buyer wants to brag or feel good about the great deal she negotiated. Every seller wants to get the maximum price for what is being sold. Countering the first offer allows buyers and sellers to feel they have influenced the deal in their favor. When either side gives up a little, the other side feels they have gained a lot.

Between honest sellers and buyers, a counter is never an insult. Don't get insulted or angered by any counter, regardless of its nature. Getting upset clouds your judgment, makes the deal personal. It's just business. (In some bazaar-based cultures, to not make a counteroffer is considered to be a grievous insult.) If you don't like the other side's counter, simply re-counter.

"Sell high and buy low" is one of the many

business clichés that sounds good, but helps not a whit. When sellers and buyers come to an agreement after some back and forth counters, then the seller sold high and the buyer bought low.

Don't immediately take the first offer. It will upset the offerer. Counter and count the money.

· XLVIII ·

Muddy Boots Are
Money Boots

*M*uddy boots are evidence that the wearer was out in the field working. Working in the field means meeting customers, visiting facilities, reviewing suppliers, solving technical problems, planting seeds, harvesting crops, doing market research, doing store checks, stocking shelves, studying competitors, drilling for oil, arguing a case, building a chimney, removing an appendix, opening the doors, interviewing a candidate, trading a stock, making a sale. It's out there, out of the office, where the money is made. Out there is the land of ideas, inspiration, facts, insights, opportunities. Out there it is muddy, bloody, tough, exhilarating, fearsome.

Because it's rough and tumble out there, desk jockeys have a million reasons to not go.

Muddy boots have many kin. People out there have scarred briefcases, callused hands, big gas bills, frequent flyer miles, luggage-tag-festooned bags, multi-stamped passports, appointment-filled calendars, bulging order books.

Customers say yes to a salesperson five times more often than to a mailed-in proposal. Reading a performance review is not a substitute for watching someone in action. Visiting the battlefield is the antidote to self-serving progress reports. Being out there is no guarantee of success, but one thing is certain: The hunter will not get his quarry if he doesn't leave the cave.

Get a pair of boots. Get them muddy. Muddy means money. Wear them out. Get a new pair.

XLIX

No

"Unintended Consequences"

"**U**nintended consequences" is the highfalu-
tin, sophisticated-sounding buzzword used
by some decision makers to dodge responsibility
for bad decisions. "Unintended consequences" is
meant to imply that the bad outcomes of a bad decision were beyond the control of the decision
maker(s). "Unintended consequences" is a de-
flection, a diversion, a glib ploy masquerading as
some kind of management reality. The phrase is
tossed around as if "unintended consequences"
are acceptable and inevitable. "Unintended consequences" are neither acceptable nor inevitable.
Consequences may be unintended, but they are
rarely unforeseeable. Smart people thinking hard

about potential, unexpected negative outcomes of a decision will identify most, if not all, "unintended consequences." Smart people must ask themselves and others, what could go wrong, what are we not anticipating, what is our worst nightmare? If smart people ask and answer these questions, they will identify the crucial unintentional consequences.

Honest decision makers facing huge, difficult decisions, think about consequences going out ten years. Honest small-town planners facing the decision to buy a privately owned golf course, or allow it to be sold to a retail mall developer, consider the differing impacts on traffic, additional police requirements, town character, tax base. Intellectually dishonest decision makers, who have an agenda, deliberately avoid considering the possible problematic consequences, or dismiss the probability of these consequences occurring. Do war makers, country invaders, country occupiers think deeply about the unintended consequences of their action, or do they skip that analysis because perchance it would interfere with the agenda?

"Unintended consequences" is a cop-out. Don't use the excuse. Don't accept the excuse.

Plan for consequences.

L

Never Be Late

*I*n business, in career building, being late is a big negative. Getting a reputation as someone who is habitually late decreases the chance of getting more responsibility, a bigger job. Being late signals lack of discipline, lack of planning, lack of sensitivity to others' schedules. People depend on people in organizations, and if someone is late, that person is not dependable.

Being late increases stress and tension. It is better to leave an hour too early than a minute too late. Racing to the airport, stewing in line, dragging luggage while frantically rushing to the gate is unhealthy. And if you miss the plane, you blow the deal, upset the client, miss the conference.

A group of investors was putting together a national string of summer athletic camps, where kids of most ages, and all skill levels, could, for a fee, attend to learn how to better play soccer, tennis, basketball, golf, and other sports. The investors planned to use prominent athletes and coaches, men and women, as spokespeople and name draws to entice kids and their parents. The investors were offering attractive financial packages to the spokespeople. One of the target spokesmen was a recently retired, after four seasons, NBA player. He was good-looking, well-spoken, spoiled, and prone to tardiness. He was late to his first two meetings with the investor group. At the end of the second meeting the lead investor began a quiet conversation with the ex-basketball player.

INVESTOR: "How old are you?"

PLAYER: "Thirty."

INVESTOR: "You've played basketball all your life. What are you going to do to earn a living the rest of your life?"

PLAYER: "I'm going to do stuff like this with you guys."

INVESTOR: "Who was stricter, your college coach or your pro coach?"

PLAYER: "College."

INVESTOR: "What would happen, what would your coach do if you were twenty-two minutes late for practice?"

PLAYER: "He'd be mad, and maybe make me run a couple of punishment miles."

INVESTOR: "And what would happen if you were twenty-two minutes late for a game?"

PLAYER: "He would probably bench me. Maybe suspend me for the next game."

INVESTOR: "Were you ever late for practice or a game?"

PLAYER: "Never."

INVESTOR: "Yes, you were. You were late for our last two meetings. Consider the meetings practice. You being late for practice makes me think you might be late for a camp opening, for the photo op with the kids. Consider each opening as a game. I can't ask

you to run any miles, but I can ask you to
be on time for everything you do with us.
Time is money. Fair enough?"
PLAYER: "Definitely. I'm hearing you."

The ex-basketball player was late for the next
meeting. He was dropped from consideration as a
spokesman. The player's ego did not drop as fast
as his fleeting fame (and value), but when reality
set in, it was too late.

Being late can be too late.

· LI ·

Act Like You Own the Place

*L*eaders are confident and concerned. They are confident in their abilities, in their colleagues, in their decision making. They are concerned about customers, problems, the future, the unknown, what the other guy who wants their business is plotting. Every day when you go to work, in the office, the store, the factory, or in the field, act with confidence. When you walk into the customer's place of business, act with confidence. Act like you own the place. Do not be arrogant. Be comfortable, at ease, calm, courteous. Act as if you work for the customer, because you do work for the customer.

When you walk into the office, into a meeting,

onto the stage, act like you own the place. Act as if you arc in your complete comfort zone.

If you did own the place you would also be concerned about its products, its people, its appearance. Acting like you own the place means you share all of the owner's concerns and you act upon them. You sweep the front stoop if it is covered with leaves. You turn off the lights in unused rooms. You inquire about the employees' new babies. You dial for dollars. You collect overdue bills.

Be confident. Be concerned. If you act like you own the place, you just might.

LII

Spend the Company's Money
as You Would Your Own

A company's money is owned by the share-holders. The primary purpose for that money is to invest in marketing—the getting and keeping of profitable customers—and in innovation. There are all kinds of obligations tied to the money. Employees must be paid. Suppliers must be paid. Lenders have to be repaid. Money wasted or ill-spent is money not available to get and keep customers. And no customers means no money for anything.

Companies need to get a return on the money they invest in employees and with suppliers. If a company pays an employee $100, it needs to get back that $100, plus a few hundred dollars more from the employee's work. If a company invests $1,000 in advertising, it needs to get, say, $10,000 in additional sales.

Companies are not glass buildings. They are collections of people. And it is those people who decide how money will be spent, and it is those people who spend the money or who authorize the spending.

In a household the spending of money should be honest, prudent, planned. Money is spent for short-term needs, for the future, sometimes bravely, sometimes for fun, for education, for health, for improvements. There is thought, risk assessment, hope when big money is spent. The people who are responsible for spending the company's money should always remember that money is the tool to keep the business, like the household, viable.

Ask yourself, "If I had the money to spend, and if it were my money, would I fly first class or coach; would I stay at the Ritz or the Rotsa; would I hire Jimmy Buffett or play his records; would I have an entourage or go solo; would I buy high-quality paint or cheap whitewash; would I take on debt to buy time to make it, or not?"

There are no perfect answers. But treating company money as your own is a good rule to use as you decide on spending.

Spend the company money as you would your own, and you and the company will have a lot more.

LIII

Don't Give the Jewish Guy
a Pork Roast

Culture. Ethnicity. Religion. Background. Politics. Causes. Relationships. Some people care passionately about these issues (and uncounted others), whereas their next-door neighbor, or next-office colleague, cares not a bit. It is okay if good people don't care about the cares, concerns, and causes of others. But it is not okay to intentionally or unintentionally be ignorant or dismissive or judgmental about matters of importance to others.

Every year, and for several years, the owner of a small business gave employees, customers, key partners, and important suppliers a holiday gift. The gift was a crown pork roast complete with stuffing. The roast was always a big hit with everyone. One of the newer employees was Jewish. Somewhat aware that people of the Jewish faith observed varying degrees of religion-based food laws, the owner asked the Jewish guy if a pork roast was an acceptable holiday gift.

Wrong question! Wrong question in every aspect. The owner should not have asked the question. The owner should have done five minutes of research to find out the acceptability of such a gift.

Even without research, the question was intemperate. It put the employee in a tough spot. A yes or no answer could be inferred as ungrateful or as embarrassing by the owner. The question was dumb and dumbfounding, as it unnecessarily raised the question of religion in the workplace (a no-no), and it subtly suggested that the Jewish guy was somewhat of an outsider, not mainstream.

The Jewish guy came to realize that the owner was not completely dense, was not prejudiced, just refreshingly oblivious to the age, gender, sexual orientation, or religion of any employee. One year later the team was going over the list of who should get or not get the traditional holiday gift.

"Any suggestions?" asked the owner.

"Yeah," said the Jewish guy. "Don't give the Jewish guy a pork roast."

A second of silence, then the owner laughed aloud. "Thank you, sir," the owner said. "No pork roast to you. You get the chocolate mousse cake. That will save us forty bucks."

"Boss man," said the office manager, "you have got to go to sensitivity training."

Looking dumb and dumbfounded, the owner quipped, "Don't tell me chocolate is also forbidden." Everyone rolled their eyes.

Don't ignore customer complaints. Don't dilly dally in responding to customer requests. Don't dismiss colleagues' ideas and suggestions. Don't downplay the differences among people. Don't pooh-pooh what is minor to you, but major to others.

And don't give the Jewish guy a pork roast.

LIV

You Can't
Unsour the Milk

Bad things happen. Some bad things, like hurricanes, are uncontrollable. And people make mistakes. You make a mistake. A new technology threatens to make your job obsolete. Your best salespeople bolt or die. One of your colleagues loses his temper with a rude but immensely important customer. Your shipment to the customer arrives late, arrives damaged, never arrives. You are in the dairy business and every bottle of milk sold to Foods-Ain't-Us is sour. When calamities happen, there is one thing you can't do: You can't unsour the milk.

You can't put sugar in the milk. You can't go back in time. You can't prevent what has already happened. You can't change the past. You can't wish the event away or wail it away. And you can't quit.

You must counterpunch. Do not waste time bemoaning your troubles. Save any blaming or self-flagellation for later, much later, if ever. Start thinking. Think hard. Assess damage. Then start counterpunching, start working, start doing. After Hurricane Katrina, officials in New Orleans and Baton Rouge hid, shirked, moaned, whined, blamed, complained. Officials in Biloxi and Mobile thought, planned, made calls, pulled on their boots, picked up their shovels, and went to work. Biloxi and Mobile were quickly back in business. Fabulous New Orleans will be back, but it won't bounce back. New Orleans will stagger back as its officials point fingers, wring their hands, and sing the blues.

When an employee develops a bad attitude, for whatever reason, it is hard, if not impossible, to fix. A bad attitude is sour milk. To try to un-sour the milk is "bad ROT," bad return on time. Part ways, and go forward.

Knowing the milk is sour, and immediately accepting that the milk is indeed sour, frees you up to leap from anxiety to action. Call the people impacted. Explain your action plan. Ask for help. Ask for new deadlines, terms, conditions. Get something done—biggies and littles—every day. Don't paralyze. Don't hunker down. Don't feel sorry for yourself. Get up at dawn's early light and do something.

Sour milk is bad. Sour grapes is worse.

LV

Get Your Product
Banned in Boston

"**B**anned" means forbidden, illicit, illegal, not allowed, not permitted, taboo.

The expression "banned in Boston" was coined after a moralist named Anthony Comstock succeeded in getting laws passed that allowed and encouraged Boston city officials to ban from the public any commercial product, book, play, or movie that they thought was offensive or unacceptable. The Comstock Law was passed in the late 1800s and wasn't completely erased until a number of Supreme Court decisions in the 1950s and 1960s reaffirmed freedom of expression and freedom of commerce.

Getting "banned in Boston" was always news.

The resultant publicity for a product banned in Boston was priceless. Products banned in Boston sold big-time everywhere else. Getting banned in Boston was such a boost to sales that commercial distributors would falsely claim that their product had been awarded the notorious appellation.

Boston doesn't ban anymore, but other places and organizations do ban. And the banners never get it. Banning a product advertises the product and increases consumer awareness and demand. Getting banned is good for business. On a per capita basis, alcohol consumption was at its highest in the United States during the Prohibition era. Huge fortunes were made by people who dared to distill, smuggle, and sell what was one day legal, then illegal, then legal. And getting "banned in Boston" or in Florida or California has sold more tickets to more plays and to more movies than have all the ads in the *Boston Gazette*.

Good sources of "bad" word-of-mouth advertising that sells include self-appointed protectors of morality, broadcast personalities who rant, politicians who pander, and the blogosphere. If you can somehow get your legal product on a big-voice mainstream public verboten list, your product is going to sell. And if it's a good product it will sell a ton. If you can get an inflammatory word into the tin ear of the right moral crusader, your advertising budget problems may be over. Let the crusader sell your product. It is perfectly all right to influence these influencers to sell your products. No harm is ever done. Good people don't need "better" people to tell them what is right or wrong. Bad people don't care if something is wrong.

Here are just a few of the products and works of humans deemed by other humans to be unacceptable in the eyes of God:

- The automobile
- Legal steroids
- Ivory
- Perfume
- Chewing gum
- The Bible
- Jukeboxes

- *The Merchant of Venice* and *King Lear*
- *The Sun Also Rises* by Ernest Hemingway
- *A Streetcar Named Desire* by
  Tennessee Williams
- *Oedipus Rex* by Sophocles
- *The Crucible* by Arthur Miller
- Oodles of paintings
- The *David* by Michelangelo
- *Alice in Wonderland* by Lewis Carroll
- Martin Luther's writings
- The Harry Potter books
- *Ulysses* by James Joyce
- Galileo's theory of the universe and the sun
- Rock 'n' roll
- Countless songs, including tunes by
  Elvis Presley and Bob Dylan
- "Little Red Riding Hood" (very evil)

Mark Twain was elated when, in 1885, the Concord, Massachusetts, public library banned *The Adventures of Huckleberry Finn*. Twain told his publisher to get the word out, as that banning would increase sales by twenty-five thousand books. Astonishing, but true, a century after publication, every once in a while, in places including the Brooklyn Public Library, Washington, DC, and New Haven, Connecticut, someone of small mind and big mouth still makes Mark Twain yuk-yuk when young Huck is once again uselessly rebanned.

These nasties below were not only banned, they were burned . . . in public. Burned in public is perfect public relations.

- *Brave New World* by Aldous Huxley
- *Catcher in the Rye* by J. D. Salinger
- *To Kill a Mockingbird* by Harper Lee
- And, of course, *Huck Finn*

"Excuse me, Mr. Banner, could you please hold the book cover close to the television cameras? Be sure people can read the title. That's it. Good. Hold the book steady. Perfect. Thank you!"

Ban, baby, ban!

Rookies might wail, "My goodness. We've been banned in Boston." Pros will smile. "Thank goodness. We've been banned in Boston."

Note: A ban is not a boycott. A ban is some-one's opinion that a product should not be bought. A boycott is the deliberate consumer act of not buying a certain product. Banned is okay. Boy-cotted is not okay.

EPILOGUE

If you are burning to succeed, flash back to any page in this book. The page will be fuel to burn.

THE CONTRIBUTORS

Successful people learn from parents and mentors. Often when the lessons are being taught, or the examples are being set, young people don't appreciate or recognize the moment. But they don't forget. Later in life they come to understand, and they are thankful.

Successful people learn a lot at the family dinner table. Of course, the "dinner table" is a metaphor for any learning done at home, for learning from others, for familyness; the dinner table is, in homes that spawn successful people, as important as any school desk.

ANONYMOUS

There was more than one anonymous contributor. This is a composite profile of Anonymous. Anonymous is male and female. Anonymous was raised in what was essentially a one-parent home, be that due to death, divorce, abandonment, or whatever. There was little money in the family. Anonymous always had a summer job, and when possible, caddied or babysat or waited tables. Anonymous was a good student, was popular, played sports. Anonymous saw good things and bad things while growing up, and was smart enough to know the difference. Somehow Anonymous scraped together the money to go to college, and pursue other advanced education. Anonymous has always been self-reliant, has always done it alone, and got the big break not due to someone else's influence, but because of luck, persistence, and taking a chance. Anonymous is still married, is divorced, is remarried. Anonymous owned or ran an organization. Anonymous is retired and is still working.

LESLIE A. BLODGETT
CEO and President
Bare Escentuals

When you grow up with a single working mom who is nuclear-fired energy, who loves themed parties and holidays and celebrations, who throws herself into every event with abandon, you are watching a maestro CEO in action. If you are smart, and Leslie Blodgett is smart, you learn how to blend joie de vivre with business. If, like Mom, you are creative and have her get-up-and-go, you will go places. And Leslie Blodgett is going places.

Leslie is the CEO and chief imagineer of Bare Escentuals, the most innovative cosmetic company on the planet. Bare Escentuals has revolutionary products, and has revolutionized how cosmetics are sold. Bare Escentuals is the number-one-selling cosmetic company on television, with recent one-year sales growth of an astonishing 83 percent! Leslie, and Leslie's products, are stars on QVC, the television selling channel. Like her mom's birthday parties, Leslie's QVC parties are well-planned, unusually themed, and fun. Another Leslie marketing innovation is an annual cruise where Bare Escentuals' legions of loyal fans can experiment with new products, have a good time, and give Leslie clues that quickly turn into new products. Leslie's mother is Sylvia Abualy. She was a home economics teacher who would sew her own fashion designs. She was the ultimate "you will succeed" mom. Sylvia made sure that Leslie went to camp, to ballet, to chorus, to gymnastics, to creative writing classes . . . and that she went enthusiastically, without complaining.

Sylvia would spend one month planning a tree-decorating party or a dance party, and everyone in the family had to participate. Bare Escentuals has dance parties as well. Everyone dances for three minutes, moves and grooves, and goes back to work taking care of customers. Sylvia was the family ringmaster, the family dynamo, always busy, always working. Ringmaster dynamos run in Sylvia's family.

Everyone is invited to Sylvia and Leslie's next party. Bring a bottle of fun.

THOMAS M. CHAPPELL
CEO and Cofounder
Tom's of Maine

In 1970 Kate and Tom Chappell concocted a wacky life plan. They would quit their well-paying, safe corporate jobs and start a small business. The business would enter one of the most competitive consumer markets in the country: Kate and Tom were going to sell toothpaste and soap and deodorant. The Chappells were going to challenge some of the biggest and best-managed companies in America. The Chappells were going to convince the customers of Procter & Gamble, Gillette, and Colgate-Palmolive to give up Crest and Dove and Scope and Right Guard. Their products would be made only of natural ingredients derived from plants and minerals, and would not be sweet-tasting or have the silky feel to which millions of consumers were happily accustomed. Even wackier, Kate and Tom's small business would donate 10 percent of profits to charity, and encourage employees to use 5 percent of their paid time to volunteer in the community. Thus, Kate and Tom moved to Kennebunk, Maine; started Tom's of Maine; raised five children; donated millions of dollars of time and treasure; and sold the majority of their wacky ideas to Colgate for over $100,000,000.

Like so many people who make it to the top, Tom was a paperboy. He was an acolyte in his church, and a member of the choir. (This early influence led to Tom getting a master's in theology from Harvard Divinity School.) Tom's mother, Virginia, felt it was important that young boys be exposed to culture, and forced Tom to learn formal ballroom dancing. George Chappell, Tom's dad, felt it was equally important to play Little League baseball.

Dinner table conversation often celebrated the entrepreneur. Virginia's family members were all small business owners. George worked in the textile industry and dabbled in small business. (Kate Cheney Chappell's family origins, the Cheneys of Cheneyville, Connecticut, were originally entrepreneurs, but her father and grandfather were big insurance company men.) Virginia and George believed in charity, not just in words, but in deeds. George said, "When you're under pressure, forget your troubles for a moment, and do something for others. It helps."

After church service on Sundays, Tom had to wait while his father collected the altar flowers. "Tommy," said Dad, "we are going to drop off these flowers at Mrs. Whiten's home." And every Sunday Tom and his father would bring flowers and sunshine to shut-ins.

Tithing profits. Free recycling bins for Kennebunk. An army of volunteers. Products good for consumers, not tested on animals, good for the environment. A social conscience. Named by *Working Mother* magazine as one of the top companies for working mothers. Named by *Child* magazine as one of the thirty great companies for working dads.

That is Tom's of Maine. That is Kate and Tom.

H. LAWRENCE CULP, JR.
President and CEO
Danaher Corporation

How does one manage a ten-billion-dollar organization comprised of six strategic business platforms, that year after year grows in revenues, profits, and returns to shareholders? How does a company that makes and markets thousands of products throughout the world continuously outperform itself? For over fifteen years Danaher Corporation has been a management marvel. The success formula is neither accidental nor a secret. Danaher hires exceptional people for every job. Every person in the company understands and lives by the Danaher Business System, which is the cultural soul and performance engine of the company. The Danaher Business System (DBS) is the Danaher way. The DBS is an exhaustive set of improvement processes, values, and management tools that the Danaher people relentlessly execute in every nook and cranny of the enterprise. And Larry Culp, CEO and an architect of DBS, insures that Danaher's top-notch people stay on their never-ending quest for innovation and improvement.

Larry Culp grew up in the Washington, DC, area. Larry, Sr., was president and CEO of Culp Welding and Machine for over twenty-five years. Larry's mom, Carol, was a vice president in the family business. (Carol later earned a PhD at the University of Pennsylvania and is now a chief of psychological services for facilities operated by the state of Maryland.) Working for the family business, and listening to his parents, was excellent career preparation for Larry—so good, in fact, that it underpinned Washington College, Harvard Business School, and becoming president and CEO of Danaher Corp. while in his thirties, one of the youngest CEOs of a Fortune 500 company.

The observant person learns while working

for the family business, participating in the dinner table conversation. Small family businesses have no room for error. They cannot have waste or inefficiency. When your name is on the door, unquestioned quality is part of your brand promise. And great quality means you can price to value, not just to recover costs. Cash is the company's lifeblood. No cash, no company. This small business reality is now part of the measurement system at Danaher: Cash is the scoreboard. Larry's parents valued the hard-to-find trusted advisers, another lesson still followed by the company today. The key to success is great workers, and that means hiring and retaining only the best. Larry remembers his dad's advice to watch the folks who call in sick on Mondays: There is probably something going on. And if the something going on leads to termination, no matter the issue, "remember that anyone you fire is somebody's child or spouse or parent. Always keep that in mind."

Top talent. Measured performance. Adherence to a proven system. Exceptional customer-defined quality. Voice of the customer. Voice of Mom and Dad. That's how one leads a winning company.

JIM DONALD
President and CEO
Starbucks Corporation

Jim Donald is one of the hardest-working CEOs on the globe. He is the hands-on president and CEO of Starbucks, who, when he makes one of his hundreds of store visits a year, immediately dons an apron and serves customers, listens to customers, and listens to Starbucks partners (employees). ("My mother wore an apron. I can wear an apron!" he says.) Jim travels the world, masterminding Starbucks' international expansion, including a massive effort to make lattes and doppio espressos the beverages of choice in China. Jim starts before dawn, wastes no time, sends and receives two hundred e-mails a day, gets much done. Jim got his work ethic from his hardworking mom. Jim's mom, Joyce, was his CEO role model. Joyce was the family CEO; she single-handedly raised Jim and his sister. The family dinner table was Joyce's boardroom. Gathering for dinner was one way Joyce pulled the family together.

Like all good CEOs Joyce set the example, expected performance, and kept the household going in tough times. She shielded her children from the many heartless goblins that plague working-mother households. Like all good CEOs, Joyce was unflappable in the face of all that was dire. She was a jack-of-all-trades. She was the family's chief strategist, visionary, coach, and counselor. A lesson learned from his mom that Jim practices every day is that the best investment of time is making sure that every individual in the organization (family) is given every opportunity to succeed.

So, if you are a Starbucks partner, a Starbucks customer, or a Starbucks stakeholder, and you see a guy in an apron, it might be Joyce's Jim. Be you so lucky!

KENNETH J. FELD
Chairman and CEO
Feld Entertainment, Inc.

The next time you see a thousand concertgoers waving candles and lighters to encourage an encore, think Irvin Feld. The next time you see a big-time rock 'n' roll tour bus blow by you on the highway, think Irvin Feld. Irvin Feld invented the concert tour! Irvin Feld would ask his son Kenneth, then a teenager, and Kenneth's sister, Karen, what they both thought of bands such as Buddy Holly and the Crickets, and what they thought of pre-released records such as "When a Man Loves a Woman" by Percy Sledge. Irvin Feld actually listened to Kenneth and Karen's opinions, and booked both Buddy Holly and Percy Sledge to concert tours. (Percy's classic hit went to number one.)

Irvin Feld bought Ringling Bros. and Barnum & Bailey circus in 1967, and the irrepressible showman staged the signing ceremony in the Colosseum in Rome! After Boston University, Kenneth went to work for his father. During the day Kenneth was side-by-side with his father, listening to Irvin's every word, carrying Irvin's briefcase. During dinnertime Irvin would rehash every moment of the business day. Kenneth was getting an MBA. Irvin Feld, who raised Kenneth and his sister by himself, would sit at the table, smoke a cigar, sip a cognac, and utter one gem of wisdom after another. "Kenneth," he would say, and say a thousand times, "All you have is your reputation, your word. Be a man of your word and you will be successful."

Irvin Feld taught not by lecturing, but by asking questions and telling stories. Irvin would ask, "Would you like me to tell you why I did that?" In the Jewish tradition, a rabbi is a teacher, and to Kenneth, his father was the greatest rabbi, the greatest teacher ever.

Kenneth succeeded his father in 1984 as chairman and CEO of Feld Entertainment, Inc., the world's largest live entertainment company. Under Kenneth's leadership the company has grown exponentially. Approximately 25,000,000 people a year have a magical experience at Ringling Bros.

and Barnum & Bailey, Disney on Ice, Disney Live!, and the Doodlebops Live!

Like his father, Kenneth is an entertainment impresario. Like his father, Kenneth was inducted into the International Circus Hall of Fame. Like his father, Kenneth is passing on entertainment wisdom . . . to his daughters Nicole and Alana.

Rabbis. Impresarios. Fathers.

CHARLIE MICHAELS
President
Sierra Global Management, LLC

"Dinner conversations in my parents' house, and my home, were ever interesting, even to a twelve-year-old. Looking back, dinner provided a better education than school," says Charlie Michaels, cofounder of Sierra Global Management, one of the country's leading European equity investment management firms. It is obvious why Charlie's firm is so expert and successful at investing in European companies: He grew up in Europe, had to write "trip reports" on adventures in Europe, and was informally prepped by a Renaissance-man father and a European mother.

Christa Michaels was a World War II refugee who became a ballerina and danced for the Swiss Ballet in Lausanne, Switzerland. As fit as any athlete, fluent in many languages, and a world traveler, Charlie's mom always has interesting things to say . . . in French, Italian, Spanish, German, and Californian. The senior Mr. Michaels, Chuck, is a true left brain/right brain guy. He's written numerous books and short stories, paints abstracts, studied writing and painting in Paris, and was a civil engineer in Germany, Libya, Italy, Spain, England, and the U.S.

Conversation at the Michaels family dinner table was a blend of science and history, of mathematics and art; it covered the country where they lived, and the world at large. And it was at the dinner table where Charlie and his sister talked about their "trip reports." When, for example, Charlie visited Siena, Italy, he was expected to write an essay on the town, the people, the food, and what he learned there. Charlie felt burdened by those reports then, but enlightened now. They were, he says, great preparation for someone who would go to Berkeley, get an MBA from Columbia, and invest in Europe.

In his spare time, Charlie goes biking in the Sierras, in the Italian Apennines, and in the Spanish Picos.

DICK PECHTER
CEO, Pershing LLC (Ret.)
Board Member, Donaldson,
Lufkin & Jenrette (Ret.)

During his travels from Yale to Harvard Business School (where he was a Baker scholar), to joining Donaldson, Lufkin & Jenrette (DLJ), to becoming treasurer, CFO, and CEO of Pershing (DLJ), to becoming chairman of DLJ Direct, to becoming a board member of DLJ, Dick Pechter learned a lot. He also learned a lot growing up in Altoona, Pennsylvania, listening to his mom and dad, Shirley and Fred. Shirley's family owned a small, struggling business that Fred took over in 1953. Fred spent the next forty years of his life as chairman and CEO, building the company to one that grossed over $20 million in sales and employed 100 people.

Intentional or not, the Pechter home was another classroom for Dick, and a good one. The virtues of studying hard, working hard, doing good for people, and giving back were manifest. The CEOs of small businesses are often the most important people in the lives of their employees, and Fred and Shirley accepted that responsibility. Fred passed away at eighty-three, still actively engaged in running his family business.

First you learn, then you teach. After DLJ, Dick taught ninth-graders in a public high school in Jersey City. First you get, then you give back. Dick is on the board of Teach for America, the outstanding organization that gets high-achieving college graduates to volunteer two years of their lives to teach inner-city kids. To date, 17,000

people have improved the lives of 2,500,000 students.

Dick Pechter is still at the head of the class.

JACQUES PÉPIN
Chef, Author, and Television Personality

Jacques Pépin is the author of twenty-four best-selling cookbooks, is a member of the James Beard Foundation's Cookbook Hall of Fame, is a Day-time Emmy Award winner (with the majestic Julia Child), a recipient of the French Legion of Honor, and a good guy. Jacques is a cook.

Jacques' father, Jean-Victor, was a cabinet-maker, but it was his mother, Jeannette, a restau-rateur, who made Jacques a great cook and a wonderful teacher. And that was because Jean-nette was a wonderful teacher.

Every morning, at 6:00 AM, in Bourg-en-Bresse, a little town near Lyon known for having the best chickens in France, ten-year-old Jacques

would walk the open market with his mother. He would listen as Jeannette appraised the vegetables and fish and fowl for sale. You get a big-league education on food and value and the economics of a restaurant listening to a canny businesswoman while walking a one-mile-long market. If you listen, you get a second education on buying, pricing, negotiating, and menu planning as you walk the one-mile return. Not many little boys love 6:00 AM marches, but all successful big boys look back with thanks. Jeannette taught Jacques to love food, to love cooking and serving food, and to love the dinnertime ritual of eating and talking.

Dinner has always been gathering time for family or for business. Dinner is the time to sit down and slow down. For Jacques and his family, dinner is a ritual: a time that demands good food, good wine, good conversation. It is a time to get to know business partners. Good food creates a receptive mood. Good food seduces people into good deals. No one knew this better, as Jacques reminds us, than Charles Maurice de

Talleyrand-Périgord. When Talleyrand was juggling Napoleon and Louis XVIII, trying to restore France to glory at the Congress of Vienna in 1814, and things were going poorly, he famously ordered, "No more advisors. We need more cooks and more pots." Talleyrand and his chefs won the day for France.

Bon appétit. À vôtre santé!

JOHN QUELCH
Professor and Senior Associate Dean
Harvard Business School

John Quelch remembers the day well. His mentor, Harvard Business School's legendary marketing scholar, Professor Theodore (Ted) Levitt, walked into John's office and asked, "What are you working on?" John said, "Marketing communications to motivate adoption of preventive health care programs." "Forget it," advised Prof. Levitt. "You must think broader. You must work on important things that are important to important people."

Senior associate dean and professor at the Harvard Business School, John Quelch has made this advice a work-shaping motto. Twenty books, over a hundred articles, and numerous case studies are bona fides for John's leadership in global marketing and business development. John's case study on the "Loctite Bond-A-Matic 2000" is one of the best-selling industrial marketing case studies in history. In addition to writing, teaching, and consulting, John is chairman of the Massachusetts Port Authority. Prior to his present position, John was dean of the London Business School.

Two hours at dinner with Ted Levitt was an unforgettable experience for John. Levitt's eloquent question, "What business are you in?" inspired hours of creative conversation. Levitt was monumental (he passed away, at eighty-one, in June 2006). He was a breakthrough marketing thinker and former editor of the *Harvard Business Review*. Levitt's classic *HBR* article "Marketing Myopia" generated over 850,000 paid reprints, and untold millions of pirated copies.

John Quelch eulogizes him best: "Ted Levitt was the most influential and imaginative professor in marketing history."

Important things that are important to important people.

PAUL SA
CEO
Stanship Incorporated

By the age of six, Paul Sa could speak Chinese, Japanese, and English. This was because his mother, Hwei Ching Nieh-Sa, daughter of a Chinese warlord and sister of a Chinese army general, had the vision and toughness to move her family from war-ravaged China to Japan. Two years after moving to Japan, Paul's mother had the foresight to send her Chinese-born six-year-old not to a Chinese school, not to a Japanese school, but to the American school. Instead of being stuck for a lifetime under Communist rule, Paul Sa was able to go to

Rensselaer Polytechnic Institute in New York, and Harvard Business School in Boston.

Paul's father, Yun-Cheng Sa, was educated in Shanghai, established the Tokyo office for the China Merchants Shipping Company, and moved to New York City in 1974, where he established the Cosmos Marine Development Corporation. Paul is forever grateful to his mother, whose prescience got him to America. Paul is forever grateful to his father, who mentored and guided Paul into the shipping industry. Paul is the CEO and owner of Stanship Incorporated, a shipping company with a fleet of bulk carriers. He is also chairman of the American Steamship Owners Protection and Liabilities Insurance Company.

Generational success is understandable, if not a given, when the character-shaping Sa family dinner table conversation was always a mélange of *isms*: the failure of Communism, the promise of capitalism, the spirit of entrepreneurialism, and the ever-forward-looking optimism.

Zhu ni hao yun!

GEORGE M. STEINBRENNER III
Principal Owner of the New York Yankees

It can be argued, albeit whimsically, that if you love Rome, then you love the preservation of its antiquities, and that if you love Shanghai, then you love the encouragement of entrepreneurs, and that if you love New York City, then you love the rescue and restoration of the New York Yankees. Whether you love the Yankees or love to hate the Yankees, you do love that the team attracts millions of spenders to NYC. You do love that the greatest brand name and logo in the history of world sports are once again shiny jewels in New York's crown, in America's crown. The Yankees' return to glory days is due to George Steinbrenner.

Ah, George Steinbrenner. The Boss. The most scrutinized and criticized and vilified owner of any sports team in existence. (Quick: Who owns the Edmonton Oilers, the St. Louis Cardinals, Manchester United, the Boston Celtics?) George Steinbrenner: the firer of the beloved, the hirer of the behated. And the man who individually saved the Yankees from the abyss of corporate clutchery and restored the majesty that Ruth and Gehrig and DiMaggio and Mantle and Maris and Huggins and McCarthy created.

George Steinbrenner's parents led by example, not only at breakfast, lunch, and dinner, but also in the way they conducted their daily lives as individuals and as a married couple. Their parents taught George and his sisters the value of hard work and entrepreneurship. The Steinbrenner children sold eggs and chickens to neighbors. As the oldest, George was in charge of bookkeeping, and precise record keeping was expected and inspected. There was a high standard of achievement in the Steinbrenner household.

George Steinbrenner's mother was the archangel of the community. Rita O'Haley Steinbrenner had compassion and kindness for everyone, and was universally loved. She taught that being in a position to be charitable to others was a gift.

Henry G. Steinbrenner II, the Boss's father, graduated from MIT with honors, was a nationally ranked track star, a visionary businessman, and a warrior. The elder Steinbrenner was an entrepreneur and a dinner table teacher. Although a strict disciplinarian, he never raised his voice. He taught his children never to give up. George Steinbrenner quotes his father and General George Patton. But George Steinbrenner would pick his father first to stand beside him in a foxhole.

George Steinbrenner was also a college track star, is a visionary and an entrepreneur, and has won more battles than Maximus Decimus. George Steinbrenner has made New York better and we are all bettered by that.

Go, Yankees!

WARD J. "TIM" TIMKEN, JR.
Chairman
The Timken Company

The Timken Company (of Canton, Ohio) was founded in 1899 and is one of the world's great and good companies. Its bearings, steel, and industrial products are manufactured and sold across the globe. It is a company that continually pulls off the rarest of organizational feats: It maintains continuity and stimulates change at the same time. The glue to the continuity is the Timken family and their adherence to the guiding principles of founder Henry H. Timken (1831–1908). That the Timken Company embraces change was well expressed by President Ronald Reagan who, upon visiting a new Timken factory, said, "I've seen the future."

The corporation is now led by Ward J. "Tim" Timken, Jr., the fifth generation of Timkens to shepherd the company. Tim is chairman of the board. He also serves on the boards of several organizations, including the Ohio Business Development Council and all of the family's philanthropic foundations. (The Timken family adheres to another Henry Timken principle by allocating a major portion of its philanthropy to communities where the company has a factory.)

When you grow up in a family that for over one hundred years has been custodian and steward of an enterprise with hundreds of thousands of employees, shareholders, stakeholders, and customers, dinnertime is a time to listen, to learn, to get ready. According to Tim, "My family is committed to our core values, which are ethics and integrity, quality, innovation, and independence. I've heard these lessons at Thanksgiving dinner at my grandfather's house, and he heard them from previous generations. We believe that family participation in the business is what maintains the continuity and consistency of vision. For example, this is a quote from my great-great-grandfather, Henry Timken, and we live by these words today."

> To be successful you must be independent. If you want to lead in any line you must bring to it independence of thought, unfailing industry, aggression, and indomitable purpose. If you have an idea which you think is right, push it to a finish. Don't let anyone else influence you against it. If we all thought the same way

there would be no progress. But above all don't set your name to anything you will ever have cause to be ashamed of.

It is refreshing and remarkable that in a business world awash with mission statements and value statements, most of which flood out with the first storm tide, there is a company that actually means and does what it says, and has been doing so for over one hundred years. It is remarkable that one family has found the way to pass its wisdom and sense of purpose so effectively from generation to generation to generation. One of those pass-on ways is collegial family dinners.

Please pass the wisdom, but hold the gravy.

WILLIAM M. WALKER
President
Walker & Dunlop, Inc., and
Green Park Financial

When your college makes it into the NCAA lacrosse tournament, and you run onto the field at a place far from home, and the only fan for your team, sitting in a driving rainstorm, is your father, another business lesson is learned. Family comes first. Mallory Walker, a veritable "who's who" in the real estate industry, had canceled all meetings and flown from Washington to Rochester (via La Guardia Airport), to get drenched and surprise his son Willy.

Twenty years later Willy Walker is the energetic, forward-thinking president of Green Park Financial and Walker & Dunlop, two of the country's premier real estate financial services firms (located in Bethesda, Maryland). Willy has a Harvard MBA, is a member of YPO (Young Presidents Organization), is chairman of the board of Transcom Worldwide S.A., is a trustee of the 112-year-old Pomfret School, and ran the Boston Marathon in two hours and thirty-six minutes.

Willy's mother is Diana Walker, the renowned photojournalist who documented the public and private lives of Presidents Jimmy Carter, Ronald Reagan, George H. W. Bush, and Bill Clinton. She was *Time* magazine's White House photographer and has earned journalism's highest awards, including first prize from World Press Photo for her shot of President Bush with U.S. troops in Saudi Arabia. Her work appears in the National Gallery, the Art Institute of Chicago, the National Museum of Women in the Arts, and the Minneapolis Museum of Art.

An accomplished family still accomplishing. Willy has three little lacrosse players and is perfectly happy to sit in the rain to watch a game.